ART OF THE WORLD

NON-EUROPEAN CULTURES

THE HISTORICAL, SOCIOLOGICAL

AND RELIGIOUS BACKGROUNDS

THE ART OF CENTRAL ASIA

BY

BENJAMIN ROWLAND

CROWN PUBLISHERS, INC., NEW YORK

Frontispiece: Buddha preaching to a Group of Disciples. Wall painting from Shrine M. III at Mirān, Chinese Turkestan. W. 39 in. 3rd century A.D. *Museum of Central Asian Antiquities, New Delhi.*
This is one of the few fragments of wall painting that Sir Aurel Stein was able to salvage from the zone of narrative scenes above the dado of Shrine M. III. Beyond the fact that the panel represents Sākyamuni preaching to a congregation of monks, there is no identifying to precise episode from the Buddha's career. Sākyamuni is distinguished by a light yellow-rimmed nimbus. All the heads are of a Western, somewhat Semitic, type. In the heads of the disciples, warm gray shading contrasts with the rosy complexions to give a powerful suggestion of relief. Highlights are applied in a heavy white impasto.

German translation © 1970 by Holle Verlag G.M.B.H. English edition first published in the United States in 1974 by Crown Publishers, Inc.

Library of Congress Catalog Card Number 74–798668.

Printed in Holland.

LIST OF ILLUSTRATIONS

7

Figures 2–12, 16, 26, 32, 47, 52, 58–61, 64, and 65 were drawn by R. Dworschak, Dilsberg; figures 13–15, 17–25, 27–31, 33–45, 49–51, 53–57, 62, 63, 66–68, and 69–80 by H. Prüstel, Mainz. The map was drawn from information supplied by the author J. J. G. M. Delfgaauw, Baden-Baden.

CONTENTS

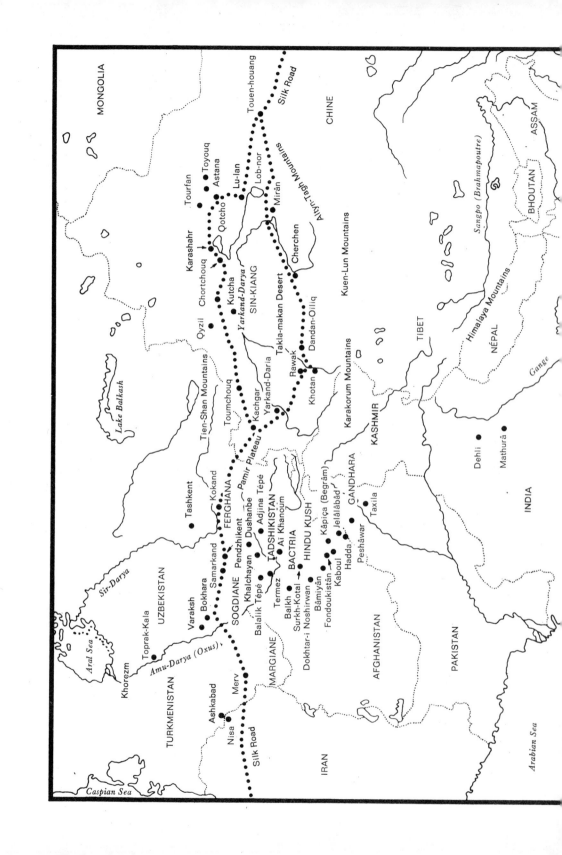

FOREWORD

Although many gifted scholars have been able to combine the functions of archaeology and art history, there are obviously basic differences in the functions and techniques of the two related crafts. Archaeologists, besides engaging in the actual work of excavating, often write acutely and perceptively on the subject of their excavations; the role of the art historian is at once less arduous but perhaps actually intellectually and aesthetically more exacting. Sir John Marshall, the distinguished excavator of Taxila, remarked in one of his running battles with contemporary art historians on the chronology of Gandhāra sculpture that the spade is mightier than the pen. The art historian is obliged to accept the data compiled in the course of scientific excavation. He cannot question the archaeologist's findings. The art historian's role is one of interpretation. It remains for him to evaluate and analyze the material on the basis of style and iconography as a revelation of the development of art in a certain region and its reflection of the social, political, and religious milieu that produced it. Part of the art historian's function is also the aesthetic appraisal of the work. He must base his judgment on the found objects as they are documented by the archaeologist, without the archaeologist's advantage of seeing them as they are dug up from their original position in the ground. If he is fortunate, he can see for himself the actual site as it remains after the excavation and restoration are complete.

Obviously, everyone interested in the history of art as an aesthetic experience and in the study of the character and evolution of styles must have the greatest admiration for the work of the archaeologist. But the art historian cannot be dismissed as a mere closet scholar, since his task, based on the training and discernment of his eye and his research into the historical, linguistic, and religious background on which his conclusions depend, is no less exacting: it attempts to give a summation of the material from both the aesthetic and historical points of view. All the advantages and handicaps which confront the art historian in the explanation and critique of ancient art forms are especially present in the study of the remote and largely inaccessible regions of Western and Eastern Turkestan.

The writer may perhaps be criticized for not including separate detailed chapters on the arts of Kashmir, Tibet, and Nepal. Although the painting and sculpture in these peripheral areas are related to certain phases of Central Asian art, these regions are geographically beyond the established boundaries of what we describe as Central Asia, and this is one reason for their omission. Unquestionably the sculpture of Ushkur and Akhnur in Kashmir is a kind of link between Gandhāra and Serindia, but at the present time the chronological and stylistic evolution of art in Kashmir is still so nebulous that it seems misleading and even dangerous to refer to it if only for purposes of comparison. Again, there were undoubtedly contacts between Tibet and Khotan at a relatively early period, and by the tenth century with eastern Sinkiang and Tun-huang. Over and beyond the problem of space and the absence of a reliable chronology, the writer is personally convinced that Tibetan art, as we know it, was from the outset such a mixture of elements of Indian and Chinese derivation that it should not properly be defined as Central Asian either in the stylistic or geographical sense. Although there were stylistic, as well as Tantric, iconographical intrusions from Tibet to Serindia, I prefer to regard Tibetan art as a quite separate sphere in the history of Asiatic art.

Except for rare and carefully selected examples, the minor arts of Central Asia cannot be discussed in our text. To anyone who has seen the enormous collections made by Sir Aurel Stein in the British Museum and New Delhi, to say nothing of the finds by German, Russian, and Japanese expeditions, it becomes immediately apparent that the treatment of this great quantity of material from every site along the trade routes is impossible within the limits of the present volume. This unquestionably valuable subject can only be mentioned when the material has some specific relationship to the monumental arts that are the subject of this book. The same omission, unfortunately, must also be observed with regard to the literally thousands of terra-cotta statuettes and decorative fragments that have been excavated in every important site from Samarkand to Turfan. Most of these minor figurines, frequently impossible to date, represent an enduring folk art, which on occasion reflects stylistic traits borrowed from monumental sculpture.

The geographical extent of Central Asia and the enormous amount of material representing successive cultures throughout this region for nearly fifteen hundred years must impose certain limitations on the coverage of the subject of Central Asian art, so that, with the exception of references to architectural monuments that have a specific connection with the plastic arts, the history of architecture must be excluded in order to concentrate on the development of painting and sculpture. In this connection, it should be noted that the basic Central Asian architectural forms are treated in Dr. Dietrich Seckel's *Buddhist Art* in the Art of the World series.

In the present work, the black-and-white illustrations, as well as text line drawings, are included not only for purposes of comparison with the subjects of the color plates but also to present material that could not be shown in the collection of color illustrations. This was done especially in the case of monuments from Russian Turkestan, in order to give adequate coverage to the art of this vital region in the history of Central Asian art. This is also the case with material from important sites such as Tumshuk: exigencies of space did not permit the inclusion of color reproductions in the text. For the background material and comparisons we have also relied very largely on line drawings in the text.

In the preparation of this volume I am primarily indebted to the great pioneers whose explorations covered the whole of Inner Asia — from the Caspian Sea to the Great Wall of China. All our knowledge of this region and its art depends on the indefatigable work of the Russian archaeologists in Central Asia, the explorations and publications by the members of the Délégation Archéologique Française en Afghanistan, and, for Serindia, or Chinese Turkestan, the incredible labors of Sir Aurel Stein, Paul Pelliot, Albert von Le Coq, and of the Russian and Japanese explores of this immense desert basin. On a more personal note I must express my gratitude to my Russian colleagues, Professor G. A. Pugachenkova, Professor B. A. Litvinskii, and Professor Alexandr' Belenitskii, for their generous presentation of otherwise unobtainable publications, for their friendly counsel, and their gracious permission to publish reproductions of material from sites in Transoxiana. In this connection a warm word of thanks is owed to my friend Grégoire Frumkin for his sage advice and support and the benefit of his universal knowledge of archaeology in the USSR. I must express my gratitude to my colleague Professor John M. Rosenfield for his continued assistance in many abstruse problems in the field, for reading and improving the manuscript, as well as for his unfailing moral support in the task of preparing my book. Finally, my wife deserves a very special expression of thanks for her untiring patience in typing large portions of the manuscript and her steadfast encouragement toward its completion.

I. INTRODUCTION

HISTORY, GEOGRAPHY, AND RELIGION

The beginning and the end of the historic civilizations of Central Asia are signalized by climactic events taking place far beyond the borders of this inner Asiatic continent. When Alexander the Great died of fever in Babylon in the spring of 323 B.C., he left as a legacy to his captains the vast conquests extending from the Hellespont to the Indus. In the Eastern satrapies of Alexander's world empire, the Macedonian's successors maintained a precarious Greek civilization in Bactria for nearly two centuries. This legacy of Hellenism they in turn bequeathed to their barbarian conquerors, the Indo-Scythian Kushans. It was precisely the formation of a Graeco-Bactrian art in this province straddling the Oxus and its perpetuation under the Kushan empire in the early centuries of our era that led to the extension of classical styles of art over all of Turkestan. The end of classical, Mazdean, and Buddhist civilization in Central Asia was the result of no less dramatic historical circumstances — happenings that live in the later histories of Iranian bards.

In the year A.D. 628, the Byzantine emperor Heraclius shattered the armies of Iran, looted the fabulous palace, the "Paradise" of Dastgard, and smashed that great wonder of the Eastern world, the Takht-i-Takdis, the Throne of Khusrau. The monarch, obstinate in his refusal to make peace, fled to Ctesiphon. Later in that burning hot summer, the veiled form of the deposed and dying Shahanshah, Khusrau II, was borne to his own treasure house, there to starve amidst riches and await merciless execution by his son Sheroe. This tragedy, so often repeated in the history of Iran, might seem to have little bearing on the destinies of Central Asia. However, with the death of Khusrau, the machinery of the Sasanian empire crumbled, its armies dissolved into ill-organized bands of provincial militia. The passing of the last great Sasanian emperor was followed by a series of short reigns usually terminating in assassinations. Within fifteen years, the followers of Mohammed, who had watched the destructive war between Heraclius and Khusrau from the Arabian sands, swarmed over Iran, and with the final annihilation of Sasanian power at Nehawand in 642, the gates of all Asia lay open to the Islamic hordes.

For centuries the European impression of the distant world of Central Asia, or Turkestan, was based on the romantic accounts of Marco Polo, who wrote at a time when the ancient cultures of this center of the Asiatic heartland had been annihilated by the Arabs and Mongols. The vague knowledge of this part of the world has gradually increased with modern research into Chinese and Arabic sources and, most of all, with the progress of modern archaeological investigation, which has in turn made possible the study of this region in its relation to art history.

The relics of the civilization that the early expeditions of Sir Aurel Stein and Albert von Le Coq resurrected from their shroud of sand give the impression of the total death of a culture, even more so than the case of ancient Egypt and Mesopotamia, so deserted and totally removed do the poor ruins appear from any ensuing culture. It is perhaps this complete extinction that makes it possible to regard Central Asia and its art with a complete objectivity and detachment. The widespread ravage of the Mongols and the effect of Islam, as well as the forces of nature, caused the Buddhist and Mazdean cultures to wither forever, stopping completely the cultural life of what must have been for centuries one of the regions of the earth most gifted in art and religion. Before this chain of fertile oases became a wasteland, its arts, as Professor Bussagli has written, revealed an extraordinary integration of "the aesthetic sensibilities of Asia and the Hellenistic Roman world and Byzantium, the Middle Ages and of Islam." [1] This is the essential theme of the present work, which is devoted to the painting and sculpture of the Central Asian world.

Central Asia, sometimes referred to as Turkestan from the domination of this region by predominantly Turkish peoples in the last millennium, can truly be referred to as the core of Asia. It is itself a landlocked continent, an area of desert wastes encroaching on fertile oases, all enclosed by gigantic mountains and steppes. This vast tract extends from the Caspian Sea to the oasis of Tun-huang in northwestern China. It is convenient to speak of Western Central Asia meaning the parts of Russian Turkestan, including the provinces, or Republics, of Turkmenistan, Uzbekistan, and Tadzhikistan, a region of steppes and desert around the orchards and fields watered by the Amu Darya and Syr Darya and their tributaries. Afghanistan north of the snow-covered peaks of the Hindu Kush and Koh-i-Baba mountain chains is geographically part of Central Asia. To the east, beyond the massif of the Pamirs, lies Eastern, or Chinese, Turkestan, the province of Sinkiang, which we may refer to as Serindia, the terrain that, in historical times, had close cultural and political contacts with both India and China. To the north of Sinkiang lie the T'ien Shan range and the steppes of Siberia. The southern boundary is formed by the Karakorum, Kuen-lun, and Altin Tagh mountains, the ramparts separating Serindia from India and Tibet. At the eastern frontier of Serindia lies China, at the end of the Great Wall. Locked within these formidable natural ramparts is the great Taklamakan Desert, an almost unbroken expanse of shifting sands bordered at its rim by narrow stretches of loess soil and stone deserts on the lower spurs of the towering hills. Tamarisk thickets and poplar forests interrupt this picture of complete desolation. Within this vast closed shell, the wasteland of the Taklamakan was girdled by chains of flourishing oases watered by the Tarim and Yarkand rivers and, before the devastation of the land by the Mongols in the thirteenth century, by elaborate systems of underground irrigation canals.

Despite its awesome circumvallation by some of the highest mountains in the world, it must not be thought that Serindia, or the Tarim basin, was entirely shut in by seemingly impenetrable natural fortifications: the passes opening through all of the encircling ranges were the gates for the trade routes which, as will be seen, were from very early times the vital arterial system connecting Central Asia with the farthest reaches of the Western and Eastern worlds.

Throughout the centuries during which civilizations flourished in Central Asia, there was little ethnic, political, linguistic, or historical unity in either the region or its peoples. The historical and artistic destinies of Central Asia were affected by the civilizations occupying or adjoining this region from the third century B.C. to the Arab invasions of the eighth and ninth centuries A.D. We have the double problem of detecting the influences of the surrounding cultures seeping into the closed Central Asian world and the evolution of autonomous artistic idioms throughout Turkestan.

It is difficult to fix the precise moment when the ancient traditions of Greece, Iran, and India first appear in this region. We may perhaps compromise with a *point de départ* of ca. 250 B.C., the moment when the Hellenistic empire, part of Alexander's conquest, began to disintegrate with the revolt and subsequent independence of the satrapies of Parthia and Bactria. Our attention will be directed to the art of the settled urban and monastic centers, and will not treat the decorative nonmonumental arts of the nomadic peoples of the Siberian steppes, who throughout this span of centuries continually threatened the cities of the trade routes and their lifelines of communication. The Eurasiatic art of the steppes, although on occasion influencing the cultures along the Silk Road, is a separate chapter in world art. In the same way, the civilizations of the Himalayan regions, Nepal and Tibet, can only be mentioned for the occasional penetration of influences from these sources into Turkestan.

Throughout every period of history the art of Central Asia has been directly dependent on the civilizations that were in geographical and historical contact with this region, notably the cultures of the Graeco-Roman West, Iran from the Achaemenid through the Sasanian period, India from Maurya times to the period of the Hindu dynasties, and China from the Han period to the tenth century of our era. Obviously, it would be impossible to provide even cursory summaries of this art-historical background of Central Asia. This material will, of course, be referred to in comparison throughout the text but it must be assumed that the reader has some knowledge of these sources or can acquaint himself with them in books devoted to these areas. In the periods that interest us, roughly from the third century B.C. until the tenth century A.D., when the entire region fell to Arab invaders from the West, there was an almost uninterrupted struggle between the nomadic hordes that moved like waves across the steppes and the settled agricultural and urban communities of Western Turkestan and the civilizations established in the oases of Serindia. These cultures could be described as stabilized, river-valley principalities sustained culturally and politically by their contacts with the great civilizations that adjoined them. Although throughout this period of nearly thirteen hundred years, there were inevitable cultural as well as military contacts with the nomadic tribes of the north, the art of these peoples who roamed the steppes from Manchuria to Hungary was essentially a simple decorative form of expression with no monumental tradition comparable to the creations of the great powers that bordered and influenced Central Asian civilization in historical times.

During the centuries of the existence of the pre-Islamic civilization of Central Asia, the very lifeblood of the many kingdoms from Khwarezm and Samarkand in the Oxus region to Kucha and Khotan on the edge of the sands of the Taklamakan was the elaborate network of underground irrigation canals. Once these systems of tunnels and ditches were allowed to fall into disrepair or were deliberately destroyed by Genghis Khan in the thirteenth century, the shroud of desert sands soon covered the skeletons of once splendid cities and monasteries. Ruin engulfed what, for a brief span of centuries, was a precarious garden of civilization in this distant lonely world. The photographs taken long ago by Sir Aurel Stein and Albert von Le Coq of once flourishing sites like Kucht and Lou-lan seem like landscapes on the moon — an endless sea of dunes with the poor broken shells of palaces and temples protruding like splintered bones from the engulfing sands. Even in the fifth century, the pilgrim Fa Hsien, embarking on his perilous journey over the roof of the world, describes the wasteland beyond Tun-huang in somber words: "In this desert are many evil demons and hot winds... There are no birds flying above, no roaming beast below, but everywhere gazing as far as the eye can reach in search of the onward route, it would be impossible to know the way but for dead men's decaying bones, which show the direction."

These continuous *déplacements* of peoples, sometimes whole nations, like the Yüeh-chih, the Huns, and, last of all, the murderous ravaging Mongol hordes, made at once for the disruption but also the renewal and variation of cultures across the Central Asian world. Anyone who has witnessed the marches of modern nomadic groups, like the Baktiari in Iran or the Hazaras in Afghanistan, will have some small conception of these ancient armies of tribesmen who shaped the destinies of the heart of Asia. It can be said, of course, that often these invasions blighted whole generations and destroyed the settled cultural centers that had been centuries in building, but, on occasion, as with the arrival of the Kushans, these interruptions led to the birth of empires.

The absence of grazing lands in Serindia did not make this territory attractive to the nomadic tribes of the steppes: their incursions into this region were always in the role of marauders or rulers exacting tribute from the settled communities along the trade routes.

The development of what we describe as Central Asian civilization in its political, religious, artistic, and, of course, commercial aspects was entirely dependent on the ancient trade routes, or Silk Road which, even as early as the third century B.C., linked China with the West. The main artery of trade from Parthian Iran passed south of the Caspian Sea to ancient Merv, where the road divided into a northern branch leading through Soghdiana by way of Bokhara and Samarkand to Kashgar beyond the Pamirs and a southern branch that followed the Oxus by way of Bactria; at Kashgar the two roads rejoined. At Kashgar the trade roads split again into trails that formed a chain around the northern and southern borders of the Taklamakan Desert to rejoin at Tunhuang. Later, another highway stretched from Soghdiana by way of Tashkent, Urumchi, and Hami to the Chinese frontier. Subsidiary roads led from Bactria (modern Balkh) through the Unai and Shibar passes to southern Afghanistan and ultimately via the Khyber and Bolan passes to India. The route from Bactria passed by way of Tash Kurgan (Sarikol) in the Pamirs, the site of the "Stone Tower" of Ptolemy's *Geography* where, it is reported, traders from East and West met for the silent barter of goods from the two ends of the world.

Our knowledge of Central Asia in ancient times is scanty and dependent entirely on Chinese, classical, and, later, Arabic sources. We learn, for example, from the Chinese annals that in or around 65 B.C. the large Scythian tribe, the Yueh-chin, the Kushans of Indian history, were driven westward from their homeland in Kansu by the so-called Huns, or the Hsiung-Nu. By 160 B.C. the Yueh-chih were established in Ferghana on the eve of their displacement of their predecessors, the Śakas, from the strategic domain of Bactria. Following their settlement in this former realm of Alexander's successors in about 135 B.C., a gradual expansion northward and southward was to make the Kushans masters of a vast empire, the Kushanshahr, extending from Chorasmia to the Bengal Valley by the middle of the first century A.D. The transformation of the Kushans from a nomadic horde into a consolidated imperium was a momentous historical moment for both the Western and Eastern worlds; and both the power and position of this new empire was destined to exercise the greatest influence on future developments in art and religion throughout all Central Asia.

Throughout the Early Han period (206 B.C.–ca. A.D. 25). Serindia was controlled by the Hunnish tribes. Between 138 and 126 B.C., the Chinese general Chang Ch'ien made an unsuccessful attempt to secure an alliance with the Yueh-chih against the Huns. As early as 60 B.C., China, with an interest in controlling the trade routes to the "Western Countries," enjoyed only a temporary dominion over Central Asia, a control, always contested by the Huns, which was consolidated into a kind of protectorate by the expeditions of General Pan Ch'ao from A.D. 73 to 78. It was he who may have repulsed a legendary Kushan invasion of Turkestan. By A.D. 130 the Chinese enjoyed effective control of the Tarim basin, and their power did not begin to decline until the third century, although, for trade reasons, various principalities like Kucha continued as tributaries of China. There were, to be sure, later sporadic Chinese conquests of the principalities of the Silk Road; the T'o-pa Tartars made Serindia a tributary by 435; Eastern Turkestan fell to Fu Chien of Former Ch'in, and Turfan was conquered by the Northern Liang armies in the middle decades of the fifth century. Kucha fell to the Tartar (T'o-pa) dynasty in 448. In 552 the Ta-chüeh (Turks) by their subjugation of the Huns fell heir to Central Asia, and in ca. 558 the same Turks, allied with Sasanian Iran, destroyed the Hephthalite Huns in Eastern Iran or Western Turkestan.

In the seventh century, the power of T'ang China asserted itself with invincible force in Central Asia, and by 635 all of Turkestan was under nominal Chinese sovereignty. Kucha and its Buddhist culture was crushed by the Chinese in 647; Khotan submitted shortly thereafter; and, with the subjection of Karashahr in 668, the independence of the Indo-European kingdoms was at an end. For about twenty years, from A.D. 670, the Tibetans made themselves masters of Chinese Turkestan, until 690, when they were supplanted by Chinese arms. In the course of the eighth and ninth centuries the Turkish Uighurs took over the oases of Kansu and the region of Turfan. The death blow to Chinese power in Central Asia fell in A.D. 751 with the annihilation of the Chinese army by the Arabs at Talas. After the tenth century all Serindia became a Muslim Turkish province.

Meanwhile in Western Turkestan, with the collapse of the Kushan empire in the mid-third century, a number of independent feudal principalities ruled in Transoxiana, even though these territories might be considered as parts of Eastern Iran of the Sasanian period. In the latter fourth century, the Chionites, successors of the Kushans, and the Hephthalite Huns ruled as vassals of the Sasanian throne in Soghdiana and Tokharistan. These tribes were finally crushed in 558 by an alliance of the Sasanians and the Western Turks. Although the territories north and south of the Oxus were nominally fiefs of the Sasanians or the Turks, it is assumed the chieftains of the various local citadels in these regions were the real rulers until the advance of the Arab conquerors brought all these lands under Islam.

The inhabitants of eastern Central Asia in the historical periods that concern us were of an Indo-European origin, perhaps the remnants of early migrations, modified by the infusion of nomadic and Turkish blood in the course of the centuries. Certainly the portrayals of the nobility of Kucha, the blond, blue-eyed knights and ladies of the Kizil wall paintings, unmistakably point to the racial affinities with the peoples of Europe. The language of this one region, Tocharian, belongs to the Indo-European, or Indo-Germanic, family of tongues. In the early centuries of the Christian Era, Khotanese was the language of trade along the Silk Road, until it was replaced by Soghdian speech and script as the lingua franca of the bridge between West and East.

The one unifying religious force in Central Asia during the historical periods was Buddhism, but, it should be emphasized, not one but many varied sects of the religion were followed in the autonomous communities from Merv to the Chinese frontier. Not only that, but throughout its history in Western Turkestan and Serindia, Buddhism was in competition with Zoroastrianism, Manichaeism, and Nestorianism as well as the pagan folk religions. A notable study of the spread of Buddhism into Transoxiana has been made by the Russian scholar Professor B. A. Litvinskii, and we can do no better than to summarize his findings. As early as Achaemenid times, Buddhism had reached Merv and Parthia and northern Russian Central Asia. According to the *Mahāvamsa*, the Great Chronicle of Ceylon, Pahlava (Parthian) and Alexandrian delegates were in attendance at a Buddhist council held by King Duttha Gamani (108–77 B.C.). In A.D. 148, the Buddhist sage An Shih-kao from Margiana, a Parthian prince who abdicated the succession to the throne, was established in Loyang as a teacher and translator of Hinayāna Buddhist texts. Another translation of Mahāyāna sūtras, the Parthian An Hsüan, was in the Chinese capital in A.D. 181. Buddhism, according to legend, was introduced to Bactria even in Sākyamuni's lifetime, and the religion was firmly established there and in Tokharistan and Margiana. Soghdian and Kushan translators of Buddhist texts were active in China in the third century.

Although it is impossible to make any general rules about the precise schools of Buddhism that flourished in Serindia, the testimony of the Chinese pilgrims, Fa Hsien in the fifth century and Hsüan-tsang in the seventh, appears to indicate that most of the kingdoms on the northern route followed the Small Vehicle whereas Mahāyāna Buddhism flourished along the southern highway. Fa Hsien speaks of myriads of priests and scores of sanghāramas dedicated to the Great Vehicle in Khotan, and this predominance of the Mahāyāna is corroborated by Hsüan-tsang. Yarkand, according to Fa Hsien, was another center of Mahāyāna Buddhism. On the northern route, however, the pilgrims tell us that Kashgar and the great kingdom of Kucha were both strongholds of the Sārvastivādins. Farther east, Karashahr was also a Hinayāna foundation. As in the case of the sites in Russian Turkestan these evidences are borne out by the archaeological material discovered at each of these sites.

Hsüan-tsang's travel notes on Buddhist foundations in Afghanistan are useful too: the community at Bāmiyān followed the Lokottaravadin doctrine, an intermediary cult between the tenets of the Small and

Great vehicles; the communities at Kāpiśa in the seventh century followed the Mahāyāna. Although the "Master of the Law" does not mention Kakrak and Fondukistan, the painting and sculpture from these convents clearly indicate their dedication to the Great Vehicle. A century later in A.D. 727, another visitor to Bāmiyān, Huei-ch'ao describes the monastery as devoted to Mahāyāna Buddhism. The same type of evidence seems to indicate that Hadda was a center of Hinayāna.

The history of the modern exploration of Central Asia begins with a number of British missions to the Kashgar region from 1834 to 1870, mainly for purposes of geographical and political reconnaissance, to be followed later in the century by Russian missions over the Tarim basin to Tibet. Although occasional manuscripts, coins, and pottery fragments were picked up by these early visitors, it was N. F. Petrovskii, Russian consul in Kashgar in the last decade of the nineteenth century, who first assembled an important collection of objects from the area. The interest aroused by his finds led to the organization of one of the first scientific expeditions by D. A. Klementz. This venture, sponsored by the Academy of Sciences of St. Petersburg, concentrated on Turfan, producing the first photographs of the Buddhist remains of Shorchuk, or Shiksim. The explorations conducted by Sven Hedin from 1898 to 1902 covered the entire Tarim basin, and he was the first to recognize the presence of Buddhist as well as Muslim antiquities in the region. In 1900, Sir Aurel Stein led his first Central Asian expedition, conducting extensive excavations in the Khotan oasis. This same indefatigable explorer conducted another memorable journey over Central Asia in 1906–09, which ended with his investigation of the Thousand Buddha Caves at Tunhuang. Stein in his last expedition to Innermost Asia, as he titled his report of this mission, conducted further excavations in the Turfan and Loulan area from 1913 to 1915. Four separate German expeditions under the direction of Albert Grünwedel and Albert von Le Coq were active in Central Asia from 1902 to 1915. These scholar-archaeologists conducted cursory excavations at Khotan and Tumshuk, but their main efforts were directed to the Buddhist remains at Kizil and the Turfan oasis. Part of the extraordinary collection of Buddhist sculpture and wall paintings obtained during these years of arduous research still survives in the Indische Kunst Abteilung of the Staatliche Museen in Berlin (Dahlem). One should not forget either the mission undertaken by the great sinologist Paul Pelliot from 1906 to 1909, in the course of which he began the excavation of the ruin site of Tumshuk and discovered the famous hidden library at Tun-huang. Between 1902 and 1909 a number of Japanese expeditions under the auspices of Count Otani Kozui and Nishihonganji (Kyōto) traveled over Turkestan more in the interests of collecting items of Buddhist interest than archaeological excavation. Further research in Central Asia by foreigners came to an end in 1915, when the Chinese forbade explorations in Sinkiang without the participation of Chinese scholars.

For our knowledge of Afghan Turkestan, that is, the parts of Afghanistan that may be described in the Central Asian orbit, we are indebted to the decades of work and publication by the Délégation Archéologique Française en Afghanistan, beginning in 1922 with the work of Foucher and continuing to the present in Bernard's excavation of the Graeco-Bactrian site of Ay-Khanum. The archaeological exploration of Russian Turkestan, interrupted by the war, has produced the most spectacular results in the last decades through the indefatigable labors of Soviet archaeologists at such sites as Toprak Kala (Khwarezm), Pyandzhikent, Balalik Tepe, Varaksha, Afrasiab, and Adzhina Tepe. These excavations, following the admirable Russian system, are the work of teams of experts, led by such distinguished scholars as Masson, Belenitskii, Pugachenkova, and B. A. Litvinskii.

The rigors of modern travel in the wasteland of Serindia, as described in the journals of such twentieth-century explorers as Albert von Le Coq and Sir Aurel Stein, are probably as nothing compared with the hardships endured by the pilgrims and traders who took this long road over Asia even before the final destruction that came with the Mongol invasions of the thirteenth century. It must be remembered, however, that in the days of Fa Hsien and Hsüan-tsang and the earlier commercial travelers, the desert had not completely engulfed the cities and monastic communities at sites like Kucha and Khotan. The oases were watered not only by the Tarim River and its subsidiary streams but also by canals. Throughout this entire vast terrain from Chorasmia to the Chinese border, as well as in ancient Afghanistan, an elaborate system of irrigation by underground tunnels (karez) sustained these islands in a desert sea. In his picturesque accounts of the modern cities of Sinkiang, which he visited in his journeys, Sir Aurel Stein frequently refers to the survival of these centers and the surrounding agricultural tracts through the maintenance of irrigation canals and to the total devastation of great areas through the failure of these systems in modern times. It is apparent that the disappearance of whole towns, castles, and monasteries in ancient times was invariably the result not only of the destruction caused by disastrous military invasions but, as has been noted above, through the neglect or deliberate destruction of the lifegiving irrigation works, which opened the way for the inevitable invasion of the desert sands.

In the following history of art in Central Asia it has become customary to assume that artistic influences, like the spread of Indian Buddhism, inevitably traveled from West to East. To a large extent this assumption is true. But we must not forget that, just as the terrible whirling desert winds — the *buran* that harassed Sir Aurel Stein on his first expedition to Khotan — blow from no predictable direction, so too the cultural forces that shaped the art of Turkestan sometimes came from many different quarters, as will be seen in at least one instance, in the counterinfluence of Chinese art in Turfan in the last centuries of Central Asian art.

Although western Central Asia, including large portions of present-day Russian Turkestan and Afghanistan beyond the Khyber Pass, were satrapies of the Achaemenid empire of Darius and his successor, for our purposes, the investigation of art in Central Asia in historical times may begin with the introduction of actual Greek forms and techniques in the colonies founded by Alexander in Bactria and Transoxiana.

The components of the art of Central Asia were drawn throughout the centuries from the cultures of peoples who adjoined this vast expanse of territory and introduced elements of their forms and techniques by trade, by tribute or booty, or by actual invasion and sovereignty over the land. The ultimate prototypes of Central Asian art are, beginning from the West, the art of ancient Iran from Achaemenid through Sasanian times, and the heritage of the Hellenistic world as implanted by Alexander's conquest and maintained for centuries by the colonist successors of the Macedonian in Transoxiana, Afghanistan, and northwest Pakistan. To this legacy must be added the contribution of the Indian world beginning with the empire of the Mauryas and continuing until the Islamic conquest in the eighth century. We cannot discount, either, the intrusion of Roman forms from the first to at least the fifth century A.D. Finally in eastern Central Asia, or Serindia, we must take into account the persistent introduction of elements from China as early as the Han period. As will become apparent again and again in subsequent chapters, no one of these foreign arts maintained its own autonomous character for long in the Central Asian environment: in every case these foreign borrowings or impositions were slowly but surely amalgamated into quite different native styles by the peoples of the widespread inner Asian continent. It is by the same token improper to speak of Central Asian art as a universal unified cultural manifestation, as one speaks of Italian or Greek art. We have to deal, in other words, not with one but many regional styles, sometimes restricted to a single small principality, and, as has been intimated, the multiple styles of these centers were invariably affected by their geographical locations and contacts with one or more sources of foreign inspiration. And, in all this, it should never be forgotten that original styles of expression develop in a native idiom.

The mention by Ptolemy of the dispatch of traders to Serindia to explore the route to the land of the Seres by the Macedonian Maes Titianus is the one ancient literary account testifying to commercial relations between the Mediterranean world and the Far East over Central Asia. It is impossible to measure the significance in the formation of styles through the importation of foreign artifacts, but there can be no question, especially in the case of an art sponsored almost exclusively by princely patrons, that the presence of examples of foreign and exotic arts would have some effect upon the taste of a given region and time. The discoveries of Roman objects in India at sites like Kohlapur and Arikamedhu need not detain us here, but the great treasure of Indian ivories and Graeco-Roman objects in metal, stone, plaster, and glass found at Begram, the ancient Kushan capital of Kāpiśa, in Afghanistan, is an illustration of the wholesale import of foreign wares to the very threshold of Central Asia. The large Roman terra-cotta vessel with Dionysian scenes discovered at Termez is a further instance of the penetration of Western art into Turkestan. Many of the gold and silver vessels of classical type found in Siberia were in all likelihood imported from somewhere in the Hellenistic empire of the West: they are the parallels and perhaps the prototypes for the handful of metal objects of actual Graeco-Bactrian manufacture. If we need further examples of the influence of imported objects to Central Asia at a later period, we have only turn to the actual fragments of Sasanian silk discovered at Astana and the precise copying of these fabrics in wall paintings from Samarkand to Kucha and Turfan.

1. Mario Bussagli, *Painting of Central Asia*, Skira, Geneva, 1963, p. 122.

II. GANDHARA

THE GRAECO-ROMAN FOUNDATION
OF CENTRAL ASIAN ART

Although Gandhāra, the ancient province comprising parts of north-western Pakistan and southern Afghanistan, is not within Central Asia, the culture of this region is so intimately related to developments in all of Turkestan that a brief description of this Late Antique art in Asia is necessary.[1] Art in Gandhāra had its beginnings with the advent of the Kushans. As has been described in the introductory chapter, this nomadic horde, the Yueh-chih of the Chinese histories, became masters of Bactria no later than the mid-second century B.C., and by the end of the first century of our era their dominions included all of Afghanistan, northwestern Pakistan, and parts of the Ganges Valley. It is possible that parts of Western Turkestan, including Chorasmia, were also under Kushan rule. Although the chronology of the Kushans remains a vexing problem, it appears that the beginning of the reign of the greatest of the Kushan rulers, Kanishka, may be dated between 78 A.D. and 128 A.D., most likely about 110–115 A.D. The dynasty of the Great Kushans came to an end with the invasion of Shāpur I of Iran in A.D. 241.

The great florescence of the school of Gandhāra must have coincided with the reign of Kanishka, renowned as a patron of Buddhism. The sculpture of Gandhāra in schist and stucco is devoted almost exclusively to the decoration of Buddhist establishments, so that its iconography is essentially derived from earlier Indian traditions recast in a classical mold. It represents a belated provincial Hellenistic style transmitted through Bactria, that is, from centers such as Khalchayan and other early Buddhist foundations in the Oxus region, reinforced by elements of style and technique borrowed from Roman art, perhaps through the actual intervention of craftsmen from the Mediterranean as a sequel to the close commercial contacts existing between the Kushan empire and Rome in the early centuries of our era. Geographically and artistically Gandhāra was a kind of no-man's land between India and Iran and the classical West. What is of primary importance for us is the fact that the technique and iconography of Gandhāra art throughout the four or five centuries of its existence provided the chief source for the various styles that developed along the Silk Road.

Fig. 1 — Gold coin of the Kushana king Kanishka, depicting the Buddha and the Greek inscription BOΔΔO. *London, British Museum. See below.*

Early examples of Gandhāra carving in the characteristic slate, or schist, reveal an unmistakable Hellenistic imprint and, with the development of the school, reflections of Roman techniques of figural sculpture and relief from the first to the fourth century. It may also be noted that in the later centuries the Indo-Roman art of Gandhāra becomes progressively more orientalized, formal, and hieratic, perhaps in response to a demand for a more abstract canon appropriate to the mystical ideals of Buddhism, also as the result of a transference to Gandhāra of the already orientalized Roman art of Palmyra and Dura Europos. In connection with the Palmyrene style of the late Gandhāra Buddhas, it is worth mentioning that provincial Palmyrene grave steles of the second century A.D. have been found at Vekil-Bazar in the oasis of Merv.[2]

The fact that a representation of Buddha appears on a coin of Kanishka (Fig. 1) indicates that such anthropomorphic portrayals of Sākyamuni were already known at the turn of the first century A.D. A typical early Gandhāra Buddha is a mixture of classical form and Indian iconography (Ill. 1). The robe is an adaptation of the toga or pallium of Roman imperial portraits to the Buddhist robe, or *sanghāti*. The head is reminiscent of the Apollo type. The wavy hair and even a krobylos are made to disguise the *ushnisha,* but *lakshanas*, the magic marks of a Buddha as described in Indian texts, such as the elongated earlobes and the *urna*, are introduced into the classical mask.

The Gandhāra Bodhisattva images, ancestors of countless representations of these beings in Central Asia, are princely figures, dressed in the finery of Indian rajahs of the Kushan period and seemingly descended from the royal portraits of Khalchayan (Ill. 3). Possibly they were intended as effigies of deified nobles. The jeweled ornaments worn by these images are of Iranian, Sarmatian, or Graeco-Roman origin, and the swallowtail convention for their dhotis appears to be a borrowing from the Neo-Attic style.

Although, as we have seen, the early type of Gandhāra Buddha has many features in common with late Hellenistic or early Roman imperial sculpture, the late examples of the Buddha type, no earlier than the third century A.D., as illustrated by the relief of the Great Miracle of Srāvasti from Pāitāvā in Afghanistan (Ill. 2), show a reversion to ancient Near Eastern characteristics. The rigid frontality and the squat proportions of the figure may remind us of Parthian art or, indeed, of that loss of all sense of beauty of proportion in Roman sculpture of the time of Constantine; and the abstraction of the earlier realistically rendered classical garment into a series of stringlike conventions, with the folds ending in meaningless forked shapes attached to the body, has parallels in the grave portraits of Palmyra (Fig. 2). A similar trend toward formalization, hieratic and dry in execution, with the drapery represented by incised lines rather than fully modeled pleats, makes its appearance in stucco sculpture as well. It is this late phase of Gandhāra art that appears to have provided models for the plaster and clay sculpture universally employed in the Buddhist monasteries of Central Asia. As we shall see in a subsequent chapter, the first translation of the Gandhāra style into a Central Asian idiom, in a union of classical, Indian, and Iranian elements, was effected in the art of such Afghan sites as Hadda, Bāmiyān, and Fondukistan.

There are several different types of relief sculpture in Gandhāra, all of which appear to reflect consecutive development in the compositional and spatial arrangements of Roman art from the first to the third century A.D. These styles of relief in Gandhāra range from the fundamental classical scheme of a number of figures isolated against a plain background (Fig. 3) to the most complicated, truly baroque, pictorial relief. Without going into a detailed analysis of this stylistic variation and evolution, it can be said that the most common type of relief in Gandhāra from the second century onward presents the figures in a deep stage or box, usually with several overlapping planes (Fig. 4), as in

Fig. 2 – Grave stele from Palmyra. Fogg Art Museum, Cambridge, Mass. See above.

Fig. 3 – Dionysian scene. Gandhara relief. B. Rowland Collection, Cambridge, Mass.
See below.

Roman carving of the Antonine period, to show the existence of the forms in a spatial ambient. Although this pictorial mode might remind us of the thickets of densely crowded figures in such early Indian reliefs as the carvings of the *toranas* at Sāñchī, the arrangement of the personages in Gandhāra panels is invariably more ordered and balanced in a classical sense, and the mode of continuous narration universally favored in Indian relief compositions rarely appears; in fact, instead of the Indian method of showing consecutive events in a story within the same frame, another adaptation of Roman practice in the narration of the Buddha legend is the allotment of a single panel to each episode in the hero's life.

The most important export from Gandhāra to Central Asia was the technique of sculptural revetment in stucco or clay for Buddhist structures and the hybrid styles of wall painting, half Indian, half classical, that flourished in these border regions. In this connection, the name of the famous site of Hadda near Jalalabad in southern Afghanistan has become almost a generic term to describe Gandhāra sculpture in stucco. Actually this lime plaster statuary is no different in technique and motifs from innumerable examples excavated at Taxila and throughout the Peshawar Valley in northwestern Pakistan, but the great variety and beauty of the hundreds of pieces recovered at Hadda by the French Archaeological Mission in the nineteen twenties attracted worldwide attention, especially with the promulgation of the theory that many of the heads of Bodhisattvas, devatās, and lay figures, in their expression of pathos and spiritual realism, seemed to anticipate the style of thirteenth-century Gothic art. Actually Hadda is beyond the confines of Central Asia proper, but the sculpture of this famous site, the ancient

Hi-lo of the Chinese pilgrims Fa Hsien and Hsüan-tsang, is of extreme importance for the development of a technique of modeling in gypsum as a cheap substitute for marble that was perfected in Alexandria in the Hellenistic period, and, from this great commercial and artistic metropolis, its use spread to Parthian and Sasanian Iran, to Transoxiana, Afghanistan, and northwestern Pakistan in the early centuries of our era. It is possible that the interest in the realistic portrayal of individual types and the radiant expressiveness of so many heads of the "Hadda" type may have already been anticipated in the Bactrian culture of Khalchayan, if, as Professor Pugachenkova has tried to demonstrate, the decorations of this palace are to be dated in the first century B.C. However, as will be explained below, it seems likely that a somewhat later date is probable. The chronology of the Hadda sculpture remains a problem: At least, the finding of Roman coins of Domitian and the fifth-century emperor Marcian by the pioneer explorer Masson before the First Afghan War presents enclosing brackets for the florescence of this monastic city, and the final terminus is supported by Hsüan-tsang's mention of the destruction of the monasteries of Nagarahāra presumably by the White Huns in ca. A.D. 450.[3]

Following a practice that became universal throughout western Central Asia and Serindia, in both the reliefs and statues attached to the walls of stupas and vihāras, the bodies of the images were modeled out of local clay around a wooden armature and covered with a thin shell of lime plaster originally painted or gilded. The heads, like the example of a "Hadda" type of devatā on Page 43, were modeled out of stucco around

Fig. 4 – Nirvana. Gandhara relief. Indian Museum, Calcutta.

a solid core of clay, reinforced with chopped straw and small stones as a binding medium. Molds were almost certainly used for the stereotyped Buddha, in which the mask is a combination of the sharpness and ideality of Gandhāra stone Buddha heads and the fullness of the Indian canon. For the individualized heads of minor deities and devotees, however, a freehand modeling technique was employed to achieve the peculiar freshness and suggestions of ecstasy and tension. It is this technique that makes so many of the Hadda heads look as if they were the last expression in Buddhist guise of the realism and passion and tension of the school of Pergamum. We may conclude that the special spiritual qualities of the Hadda stuccos is either an inheritance of the late Hellenistic Bactrian art of Khalchayan or a reflection, perhaps through the intervention of provincial Roman craftsmen, of the revival of the Hellenistic *Sturm und Drang* in Roman art of the Antonine period.

In concluding our consideration of this Asiatic phase of the Late Antique, it might be possible to think of the art of Gandhāra as just another regional style, like the autonomous modes of expression that we shall encounter in the various principalities of Russian Turkestan. The Gandhāra style was, of course, more widely distributed in a geographical sense and its production infinitely more prolific and varied, yet it has the earmarks both of a provincial late classical mode and at the same time a school in which elements of classical, Indian, and Iranian origin are blended into a distinctive independent style.

Whereas the school of Buddhist sculpture that flourished under the Kushans at Mathurā is completely Indian in character, a logical outgrowth of the earlier styles of Indian art, the sculpture of Gandhāra that flourished in the northern portions of the Kushanshahr, is, strictly speaking, dependent on Graeco-Roman stylistic prototypes. As we shall explain in a later chapter, the only artistic expression that we can really associate with the Kushans racially as well as aesthetically is the series of royal portraits and related memorials at the sanctuaries dedicated to divinized sovereigns at Surkh Kotal in Afghanistan and a similar temple enshrining effigies of W'ima Kadphises, Kanishka, and lesser princes at Mathurā.

1. The subject has been treated extensively and with great distinction by Dr. Seckel in his *Kunst des Buddhismus* in the present series.
2. G. A. Pugachenkova, *Iskusstvo Turkmenistana*, Moscow, 1967, Pl. 26.
3. The recent find of a cache of coins of Shapur III (383–388) at Tepe Shotor in Hadda would appear to provide a useful date for the florescence of the school. (M. and S. Mostamindi, "Nouvelles fouilles à Hadda [1966–1967]," *Arts Asiatiques*, XIX, 1969, p. 23.)

III. MIRĀN

LATE ANTIQUE ART IN SERINDIA

Geographically farthest removed from India and Gandhāra and yet closest in style and date to the Late Antique art of the Kushan period are the remains unearthed at Mirān on the southern artery of trade three hundred miles from the frontiers of China. This site was first excavated by the great British archaeologist Sir M. Aurel Stein in 1907, and later explored by the third Japanese expedition led by Count Otani in 1911. Mirān lies northeast of the Altin Tagh on the border of the desert of Lop Nor. The site has been identified as Yü-ni, the capital of the principality of Shan-shan in the Han period.

Describing his visit to Shan-shan and the capital Mirān, in the early fifth century, the Chinese pilgrim Fa Hsien observed that "the laity and Srāmanas of this country wholly practice the religion . . . of India . . . all use Indian books and the Indian language" — an eloquent testimony to the close, and it would seem direct, ties between this distant outpost and Indian culture.

The shrines excavated at Mirān included a temple (M. II) with fragments of stucco sculpture, among them a colossal Buddha image, and such architectural details in carved wood as a bracket capital of Persepolitan type. Two circular sanctuaries (M. III and M. V) consisted of a stupa, a tall structure raised on a number of basement stories or drums, enclosed in a round conical building, so that an ambulatory for circumambulation of the relic mound was provided between the central stupa and the surrounding wall. The entire surface of the interior wall of this circular ambulatory in both shrines was covered with mural paintings. The date of the principal mural decorations in shrine M. V and most likely the entire complex may be established by an inscription in Brahmi script of the third century recording the name of an artist, Tita, which we may perhaps recognize as a transliteration of the Latin Titus. The inscription reads: "This fresco is the work of Tita, who has received 3,000 Bhammakas for it."

In the lowest zone or dado of M. V was a continuous painted frieze representing nude putti and youthful genii wearing Iranian pointed caps supporting a thick heavy garland (Fig. 5); framed in the swags of this

PLATE P. 41

PLATE P. 41

Fig. 5 – Paintings from the lower wall area of Temple M.V. Mirān. Museum of Central Asian Antiquities, New Delhi. Compare p. 33.

wreath were painted what are presumably portrayals of male and female donors or worshipers. Busts of winged beings were enclosed by the loops of the wreath in the round temple, M. III (Fig. 6).

Above this lower register were representations of the Buddha legend, such as the fragment from the life of Sākyamuni in a style that could be described as the pictorial equivalent of the same subjects as those found in Gandhāra reliefs. The motif of busts framed in the swags of a garland, supported by erotes and, in the present example, by a youth wearing a Phrygian cap, is a favorite one in Gandhāra reliefs (Fig. 7) and ultimately in Roman sarcophagi of the early empire. The little genius

Fig. 6 – Bust of a winged genie. From Temple M. III, Mirān. Museum of Central Asian Antiquities, New Delhi. See above.

Fig. 7 Young men carrying garlands. Gandhara relief. Central Museum, Lahore. Compare page 34.

with his peaked bonnet could be mistaken for an Orpheus or a Mithra in any number of Roman mosaics and wall paintings.

No one can fail to detect the marked resemblance between the bust of the devotee framed in a wreath in our illustration and the Fayum grave portraits from Roman Egypt (Fig. 8). Both the type of male "portrait" in our detail of the Mirān dado and the cursory use of light and shade could be matched in many examples of these late Roman heads painted in encaustic; this resemblance strongly suggests the participation of an atelier of artists trained in the Mediterranean tradition

Fig. 8 – Mummy portrait from the Fayum. Formerly Graf Collection, Vienna. See above.

under the direction of Tita. We can recognize another universal cliché of Late Antique art for the expression of spirituality — literally, a "soulful look" — in the enormous enlargement of the eyes, which we encounter in the Constantinian portraits of fourth-century Rome, in the funerary sculpture of Palmyra (Fig. 12), and in the portrayals of priests and acolytes in the wall paintings of Dura Europos. This period of the third and fourth centuries in the Mediterranean world was marked by the florescence of the mystery cults, with their emphasis on initiation into the other world, so that it is not surprising that this formula for ghostly ecstasy or exaltation should have been so acceptable to the expression of the mystical ideals of Buddhism here at Mirān at the furthest edge of the dying classical world.

Stylistically the group of Buddha and his disciples from Shrine M. III reveals the same reflection of the Late Antique manner in the actual types and the reduction of the chiaroscuro to a thickening of the contour lines, enclosing essentially flat areas of tone, together with a decorative rather than functional use of white highlights. The head of the Buddha at the left presents certain unusual iconographic features, such as the moustache and the traces of an unusually large ushnisha. These attributes have a rather close parallel in a Buddha head discovered at Butkara in the Swat Valley (Fig. 9) and to the representations of Śākyamuni in the famous series of Gandhāra reliefs formerly in the collection of the Guides' Mess at Mardan (Fig. 10) near Peshawar. Indeed Bussagli has suggested that not only these isolated details, but the spatial composition of the Mirān paintings, shows such an extraordinary resemblance to the reliefs from Buner that they might be regarded as creations of the same workshop.[1] It will be noted that the brush drawing in the Mirān figures is extremely free, even cursive, in the sure sweeping lines that define the features. Touches of white are added to enhance the suggestion of relief. This is very much the same kind of linear reduction of a classical style that is found in the surviving fragments of painting at Hadda.

Among the few surviving examples of painting in Gandhāra are a small number of fragmentary decorations discovered at Tepe Kalan at Hadda during the preliminary excavations by Barthoux. The remains unearthed at this site are perhaps the earliest and most classical from this famous monastery. Their importance to the Mirān cycle is obviously as a kind of steppingstone between the Late Antique style of the Roman West and that Eastern outpost of the classical manner. The decorations included the now-faded representations of Buddha and, of special interest to us, a small niche that originally sheltered a statue of the Buddha. On the side walls are painted representations of donors holding lotus blossoms and, on the vault of the little shrine, winged erotes holding a wreath (Ill. 4). These flying cupids were, as so often in Buddhist foundations of Afghanistan, part of a unified combination of painting and

Fig. 10 — Sakyamuni meets a Brahman for the first time. From Mardan. Archaeological Museum, Peshawar, Northwest Pakistan. See above.

sculpture. The iconography of the putti supporting a garland over the head of the Buddha might be described as the "Coronation" or "Transfiguration" of Śākyamuni: it is found in a number of examples of Gandhāra sculpture of the Great Miracle of Śrāvastī and in the Gupta relief of Kārlī representing the Buddha in his transcendent aspect.[2] In the Hadda painting, the resemblance to Late Antique portrayals of erotes is notable in the still classical types, and the reduction of the modeling to a reinforcement of the contour lines has many parallels in the late Roman paintings of Dura Europos. This provincial Roman manner, the pictorial counterpart of Gandhāra sculpture, may also be noted in fragments of mural decoration from the early Kushan or Bactrian palace of Khalchayan. All of these examples of Eastern classical painting in Transoxiana and at Hadda are presumably to be dated from the first to the fifth century A.D.

PLATE P. 42
The early penetration of classical forms to the very frontiers of China is further certified by the finding of a fragment of woven textile at Lou-lan to the north of Mīrān. Represented are a head of Hermes and his emblem the caduceus in a Late Antique style closely related to other examples of such weaving found in the Roman Egypt and generally dated in the fourth century. In the classical head of the Lou-lan fragment, we have a simulation in weaving of the same conventionalized shading already noted in the Mīrān paintings. The Lou-lan tapestry is

Fig. 11 – Head of Hermes. Textile fragment. Abegg Stiftung, Riggisburg. Compare p. 39.

Fig. 12 — Head of a figure representing one of the four seasons. Barberini sarcophagus. Dumbarton Oaks, Washington, D.C. Compare p. 40.

certainly an import and not a local production; it is closely related to other examples of Late Antique woven stuffs, such as the beautiful head of Hermes in the Abegg Stiftung, Riggisburg, originally part of a large composition of Meleager Hunting the Calydonian Boar (Fig. 11). The discovery of our fragment at Lou-lan is important because of its relation to the wall paintings of nearby Mirān. The woven design is a close counterpart of the details of the Mirān murals illustrated in our Plates 1 and 2. Certainly not only the possible participation of artists trained in the Roman West, but also the presence of imported objects, such as the Hermes of Lou-lan, was responsible for the introduction of late classical styles to the oases of the Silk Road.

Turning now to the sculpture of Mirān, a singularly beautiful head of a Bodhisattva or Devatā in the collection of the National Museum in New Delhi will serve to illustrate the kinship of the plastic art of this site with Gandhāra and ultimately with the art of the Mediterranean world. The material, stucco, rare in Serindia, immediately relates this fragment to the technique of Hadda and many other sites in Afghanistan and Pakistan. The face does not have the masklike formality of so much of the Hadda sculpture dependent on molds, but appears to have been modeled freehand with a piquant realism within a classical frame close to the more Hellenistic Hadda types. By the same token we are reminded of the belated Bactrian sculpture of Toprak Kala and Khal-chayan.

It is hardly surprising that the head of a devatā illustrated on Page 42 is so close in technique and feeling to examples from Hadda and north-western Pakistan. The facial mask and hair appear to have been modeled with a consummate suggestion of the inner spiritual ecstasy that illumines the countenance of the youthful divinity. An expression of rapt wistful introspection is communicated by the heavy-lidded eyes and the small, faintly smiling lips. Again, as in stucco sculpture of Gandhāra, we have an example of the realistic Hellenistic manner diverted to spiritual ends, a type of expression that appears later in Gothic art. It should be noted how humanistic are these reflections of the Late Antique in the early period of Central Asian art in comparison to the frozen, mechanical masks of divinities at sites dating from the sixth to the ninth centuries where the classical ideal was replaced by ancient oriental and Indian tendencies to the hieratic and abstract. A single example will serve to illustrate the unmistakable relationship between the stucco sculpture of Mirān and Gandhāra. This is the head

PLATE P. 43 of a devatā or Bodhisattva from the region of Peshawar in northwestern Pakistan. Like the devatā from Mirān, the gentle androgynous face framed in ringlets reminds us of Roman representations of ephebes, or youthful personifications of the Seasons (Fig. 12), but the elongated earlobes and almond eyes are distinctly Indian features. The face appears to be a combination of a soft and free modeling, accentuated by the rather sharp definition of the brows. Here, as often in the stucco art of Gandhāra, the two sides of the face are not precisely symmetrical, a device that heightens the animation of the countenance. Probably, like the fragment from Mirān, this head formed part of a large relief, in which the bodies were constructed of local clay on a wooden armature.

In the same way there appears to be a relationship or, perhaps better, a parallel between the Mirān lime plaster sculpture and terra-cotta heads from Ushkur and Akhnur in Kashmir, believed to date from the seventh century.[3] It is obvious that both the Mirān head and the examples from Kashmir share a common heritage with the Buddhist remains from Gandhāra.

1. Mario Bussagli, *Painting of Central Asia*, Skira, Geneva, 1963, p. 23.
2. B. Rowland, *The Art and Architecture of India*, Third Edition, Baltimore, 1967, Pl. 88(B).
3. Rowland, *Art and Architecture*, Pl. 69(A).

Busts framed in a garland. Wall painting from the dado of Shrine M.V. at Mirān, Chinese Turkestan. 3rd century A.D. *Museum of Central Asian Antiquities, New Delhi.*

The motif of busts framed in the swags of a garland, supported by erotes and, in the present detail, by a youth wearing a Phrygian cap, is a favorite one in Gandhāra reliefs and ultimately in Roman sarcophagi of the early Empire. The Mirān murals were painted on stucco over a backing of clay mixed with cut reeds. Above the dado of Shrine M.V. was a monumental painting representing the various episodes of the *Vessantara Jātaka.*

Head of a Devatā from Shrine M. II at Mirān, Chinese Turkestan. Stucco. 3rd century A.D. *Stein Collection, National Museum, New Delhi.*
The fragment is part of a stucco wall decoration in high relief, a technique that can be seen in innumerable sites throughout Gandhāra and even in the regions north of the Oxus. Probably this and other isolated fragments found in Shrine M. II were parts of large stucco ensembles adjoining the colossal Buddha images uncovered in the sanctuary.

Head of a Devatā. Stucco with traces of polychromy. From Peshawar region, NW Pakistan. H. 8½ in. 3rd–5th century A.D. *Collection Benjamin Rowland, Cambridge, Massachusetts.*

This head of a Buddhist divinity, possibly a Bodhisattva, is an example of a technique employed for the sculptural decoration of Buddhist sanctuaries from Taxila in the Punjab throughout Afghanistan and the Buddhist foundations north of the Oxus. The lime plaster core was reinforced with small stones, animal hair of straw, and covered with a final layer of finely sieved plaster.

43

Head of Hermes and Caduceus. Fragment of wool tapestry from Lou-lan, Chinese Turkestan, H. 14 cm. 3rd century A.D. *Stein Collection, National Museum, New Delhi.*

The strongly classical style of this tapestry relates it to Late Antique and Coptic representations of pagan subjects. Most likely the piece was imported by traders from the West and found its way to the graveyard of Lou-lan shortly before the abandonment of that site in the 3rd century A.D.

44

IV. THE ART OF WESTERN TURKESTAN

BACTRIA AND THE GREAT PRINCIPALITIES
OF RUSSIAN CENTRAL ASIA

In the centuries before Alexander's conquest, when all the Middle East from Egypt and Ethiopia to northern India lay under the sway of the Achaemenid rulers of Iran, the ancient provinces of Chorasmia, Soghdiana, Ferghana, and Bactria formed the outlying satrapies of the empire of Cyrus and his successors. They were annexed to form bastions against the Scythian tribes menacing the eastern frontiers of Iran, and Cyrus himself lost his life in a campaign against the nomadic Massagetae. It was in this remote period that urban civilization had its beginnings with the founding of cities such as Afrasiab, the modern Samarkand, in what is today Russian Turkestan. These ancient provinces are now comprised within the boundaries of the Soviet Republics of Turkmenistan, Uzbekistan, and Tadzhikistan. Southern Bactria extended across the Oxus into northern Afghanistan, and Turkmenistan included part of the territories of the Parthian Empire of Iran.

At first glance a map of the archaeological sites in Soviet Central Asia looks like a chart of the heavens with its hundreds of sites like galaxies in the sky. Obviously in our survey of the art of Turkestan it will be possible to visit only a small number of the more important centers of ancient art in this region to represent different moments in the history of painting and sculpture from the third century B.C. to the period of the Arab invasions beginning in the eighth century A.D.

It is difficult to decide how to present the widely scattered and varied remains from the ruin sites of what the Russians describe as *Sradnyaya Aziya,* "Middle Asia." We propose, therefore, to study this material in a roughly chronological order regardless of precise geography, beginning with an account of the finds of Hellenistic art in Bactria and Parthia.

Before proceeding any further, a brief digression is imperative. Although a detailed account of Iran and its culture under the Parthian and Sasanian dynasties is impossible within the limits of the present work, it is both necessary and appropriate to present a sketchy outline of this civilization since its territories adjoined both the ancient principalities of western Central Asia and Bactria and the Kushan Empire. Chronologically the rise and fall of Parthia coincided with the short-lived florescence of Hellenic Bactria and the ascendancy of the Kushanshahr to its greatest power, a period extending from about 250 B.C. until the overthrow of the Parthian dynasty by the first Sasanian ruler, Ardashir, in A.D. 226. The Parthians, originally a nomadic people from northeastern Iran, came into power with their overthrow of the Greek strategos, Andragoras, and the gradual absorption of the territories of Iran as they existed under the former Achaemenid dynasty. In the days of the great early rulers like Mithradates I, the Parthians proclaimed themselves Philhellenes and took over the Hellenistic culture and art introduced by Alexander and his immediate successors. With their expansion to the West and their confrontation with the hostile Roman world they abandoned Philhellenism in favor of a return to national customs; in art, they reverted to ancient Near Eastern traditions, including a hieratic frontality and schematized linear treatment of the human figure that had its beginnings even before the Achaemenid period in the art of Mesopotamia. These national elements in later Parthian art undoubtedly had an influence on the art of the Kushans from Soghdiana to Gandhāra and, perhaps ultimately, on the artistic background of all Central Asia.

As a further footnote to developments in Iran it should be noted that the Sasanians (A.D. 226–651), who were even more concerned with their Iranian heritage, sought to eradicate all traces of Parthian culture that they regarded as non-Iranian. They made a conscious attempt to return to the grandeur of Achaemenid art combined with borrowings in technique and style from the Roman West. The essence of Sasanian art, as will be seen reflected in cultures beyond the frontiers of Iran, was a frozen inactivity, a symbolic rather than dramatic treatment of both figures and narrative in monumental sculpture (as in the great rock-cut reliefs of Bishapur and Naqsh-i-Rustam [1], and, especially in the sumptuary art of metalwork and textile design, a wonderful feeling for surface pattern and clarity in design and execution within a formal expression that is essentially heraldic rather than real.

The ultimate classical foundation of art in Central Asia is to be sought in those outposts of Hellenistic civilization established by Alexander in his conquest of the East. Until comparatively recently we were resigned to regard the existence of a Greek culture in Parthia and Bactria in the form of monumental sculpture and architecture as a mirage, leaving us only with the evidence of the magnificent Bactrian coins as relics of the rule of Alexander's successors. Within a decade the discoveries at "Mithridatkert," the ancient Parthian capital of Mithridates I at Nisa in Turkmenistan, and the more recent excavations at Ay Khanum in northern Afghanistan have completely changed the picture.

The finds in the palaces and shrines at Nisa included fragments of Hellenistic marble statues of Aphrodite and other divinities, and in the treasure room a collection of over forty magnificent ivory rhytons, each one carved from a single elephant's tusk (Fig. 13). Additional ivory was required, of course, for fashioning the elaborate "figure heads" of the vessels. These splendid drinking-horns, now divided among the museums of Ashkabad, Tashkent, and the Hermitage, present us with exactly that fusion of Iranian and Greek forms that we would expect at this moment of history, presumably the late third or early second century B.C. The rhytons themselves, terminating in the shapes of goddesses, ibex, lions, griffins, and other fantastic monsters, reproduce older Achaemenid shapes in gold and silver shapes (Fig. 14), and the tops or cornices of these vessels are decorated with exquisitely carved friezes of Dionysian scenes or groups of Olympians (Ill. 6). In some cases, these reliefs were surmounted by a circle of masklike faces, which immediately suggest a favorite Parthian architectural decoration in the form of human heads seen at the palace of Hatra.[2] Although the figures in the friezes of these drinking horns are clearly recognizable as Hellenistic types, they have a certain frontality and stiffness that already suggest the future course of Parthian art in its reversion to ancient oriental conventions.

So far the excavations at Ay Khanum have brought to light the ruins of a palace complex with a portico of 18 massive columns crowned by Corinthian capitals related to the Hellenistic development of this order at Miletus (Fig. 15).[3] The finds also include a number of inscriptions with Greek epigrams, together with a marble herm of Herakles from the gymnasium.[4] As M. Bernard has pointed out, the same emphasis on the training of mind and body, which prevailed at Delphi and Olympia, was transported by the Greek colonists to this remote heart of the Asiatic world.[5]

The coinage of Bactria, for so long our only record of this Hellenistic province, is at once a dynastic history in portraiture and a magnificent

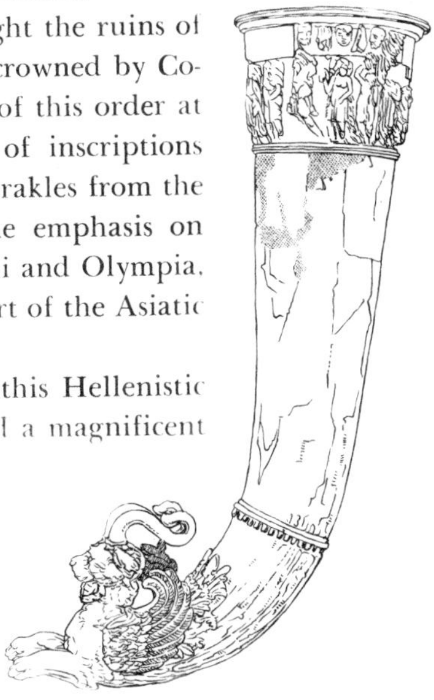

Fig. 13 – Ivory rhyton from Nisa, U.S.S.R. See above.

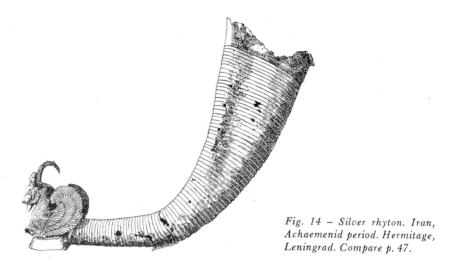

Fig. 14 – Silver rhyton. Iran, Achaemenid period. Hermitage, Leningrad. Compare p. 47.

art from in itself (Ill. 8a, b, c). The tetradrachms and staters, struck by Diodotus and his successors, are among the most beautiful coins in the Hellenistic world. The profile portraits of the rulers are as powerful characterizations as the likenesses of Seleucid monarchs in the bronze busts of Herculaneum, all marked by the greatest sharpness of execution. The portrayals of divinities, including Herakles, Poseidon, and Zeus on the reverse of these medals, appear like small-scale reproductions of statues in the style of Praxiteles and Lysippus. Whether these miniature simulacra of the Olympians were taken from cult images venerated in Bactria is a question that only the excavations of Ay Khanum and other Graeco-Bactrian districts like Parkhar in Tadzhikestan may one day reveal.

Many superb examples of Hellenistic gold and silver vessels preserved in the Hermitage have been attributed to Bactria. Some, like the partially gilded silver plate with the representation of two riders in the howdah of an elephant (Ill. 7), certainly have a convincing Bactrian flavor, since one of the riders bears a distinct resemblance to the coin portraits of Eucratides (Ill. 8c), and the workmanship of the plate as a whole seems to be a larger version of the Bactrian coins.

These scanty remnants of a true Hellenistic Greek art in the easternmost provinces of the Seleucid Empire seem to provide a background for the vital persistence of Hellenistic ideals at various sites in Bactria, even after the dynasty of Diodotus and Euthydemus came to an end with the barbarian invasions of the late second century B.C.

*Fig. 15 – Corinthian capital,
Aï Khanum, Afghanistan.
Compare p. 47.*

Although ancient Bactria has been thought of as a small principality south of the Oxus that sometimes, as under Demetreus, reached out for Indian conquests, Russian archaeologists are of the opinion that the territories and influence of the Greek satraps extended far to the north, an opinion borne out by the finds of strongly Hellenistic sculpture at Khalchayan and the examples of Bactrian metalwork that have come to light in Russian Turkestan. In writing of his visit to Bactra, or "Balach," in the thirteenth century Marco Polo describes the ancient capital as a once large and magnificent city, the reputed scene of the marriage of Alexander and Roxana. The Venetian traveler speaks of ruinous marble palaces and spacious squares, despoiled by many invaders, but still visible in his day. Of these splendors which may have gone back to the times of Alexander's successors or the Kushanas, no trace has been found.

Of extreme importance for the later development of art in Central Asia and Gandhāra is a group of sculptures in Bactria that may be assigned to the period following the disappearance of the Hellenistic dynasty in the mid-second century B.C. These would include the remarkable clay sculpture of Khalchayan (Ill. 17), the famous frieze of the Musicians from Airtam (Ill. 19), and a few examples of stone carving from the Kunduz region and the Kushan sanctuary at Surkh Kotal in Afghanistan (Fig. 34).

The ruins of an impressive castle at Khalchayan, near Denau, in southeastern Uzbekistan, contained the remains of an elaborate painted and

Fig. 16 – Terra cotta plaque depicting a king seated on a throne. From Khalchajan, U.S.S.R. Compare. p. 51.

sculptured decoration in the iwan and throne hall. Of particular interest was a monumental frieze, modeled in clay, representing members of the ruling house (Ill. 17), warriors, a cavalcade of horsemen, and an assemblage of Olympian deities, including Athena. This band of sculpture, according to Professor Pugachenkova, was placed some ten feet above the floor and, as in the carving of the Parthenon frieze, the upper portions of the composition were modeled in higher relief in order to compensate for the foreshortened view from below. Above this frieze was a zone of garland-bearing putti suggesting the same motif favored in Gandhāra sculpture and the painted dado of Mirān. The individual heads of princes and warriors display a degree of realism and pathos reminiscent of the school of Pergamum. The resemblance of some of these heads to the coin portraits of the mysterious Heraeus, perhaps one of the first Kushan rulers, has led Professor Pugachenkova to date these remarkable works in the first century B.C. It could be pointed out, however, that the Heraeus coin portrait with its large style and heavy jowls has many parallels in the portrayals of generalized Kushan ethnic types in the sculpture of Hadda, so that its value for dating the Khalchayan sculpture is somewhat diminished, especially since the resemblance in the Heraeus portrait to noblemen at Khalchayan appears to be no more than simple coincidence. It seems more plausible to date the finds at Khalchayan in the first or early second century A.D., roughly contemporary with the Kushan sanctuary at Surkh Kotal in Afghanistan and other Indo-Scythian sites discovered in the Transoxian territories.

Certainly, these ideal portrayals of the princes of Khalchayan have strong affinities with the Bodhisattva image of Gandhāra (Ill. 18) and the expressive stucco heads found at Hadda and Taxila. At the same time a small terra-cotta plaque discovered at Khalchayan with a representation of an enthroned king (Fig. 16) is closely related to the royal Kushan portraits of Surkh Kotal and Mathurā (Fig. 17).

A pioneer discovery in 1932, which led to the gradual and extraordinary excavation of the classical and Buddhist antiquities of Russian Turkestan, is the famous frieze from Airtam, above Termez, on the Amu Darya. The first fragments of this magnificent sculpture were found partly submerged along the riverbank, and the adjoining parts of the relief were uncovered during scientific excavations of a temple presumably dedicated to Buddhism. The frieze consists of some eight slabs over 100 centimeters long and 40 to 50 centimeters high. The decoration consists of busts of personages, some playing musical instruments and, as frequently seen in Gandhāra capitals, emerging from an enfolding border of acanthus leaves (Ill. 19). The subject matter, if not purely decorative, is highly problematical. The foliate motifs, stiff and somewhat formalized, immediately remind us of the familiar type of acanthus in the Gandhāra versions of the Corinthian order (Fig. 18). Although at first glance the faces of the musicians certainly suggest something of the rather masklike (Palmyrene) style of Gandhāra Buddhist sculpture (Ill. 2), a closer

Fig. 17 – Portrait statue of W'ima Kadphises. Archeological Museum, Muttra. See above

Fig. 18 – Corinthian capital from Gandhara. Indian Museum, Calcutta. Compare p. 49.

inspection suggests a much more intimate and subtle reflection, or re-working, of the classical ideal. In other words, one is tempted to agree with the opinion of many distinguished Russian scholars that the Airtam carvings represent a local Bactrian school of stone carving, probably to be dated around the very beginning of the first millennium of our era. It is very tempting to see a connection between the Airtam frieze and the limestone capitals found at Chamquala (Ill. 10), not far from Baghlan and Surkh Kotal in the Kunduz River valley of Afghan Turkestan. These capitals are carved from the same stone employed at the famous Kushan sanctuary at Surkh Kotal. Some of these architectural fragments illustrate scenes from the Buddha legend in a Gandhāran style; one, a corner pilaster capital, shown here in Illustration 10, is an adaptation of the Persepolian type, where a frontal lion on the abacus is clawing two addorsed humped bulls. Below, framed in acanthus leaves, is a half-length figure holding a casket or reliquary. Both the carving of this bust and the rather stiffly serrated acanthus leaves appear very close to the style of the Airtam panels. In one sense the Chamqala capital is a cross between the Greek figured capital and its later development into the Roman composite Order with the familiar motif of addorsed beasts of Achaemenid tradition. What we have, in other words, is the same marriage of Iranian and Hellenistic forms that characterized other monuments of Bactrian art; for example, the palace of Khalchayan built along ancient Achaemenid lines with a columnar iwan or porch on the exterior was decorated in a completely Hellenistic style of sculpture and painting in the interior apartments.

To sum up, it is probable, therefore, that the Airtam frieze and the

Chamqala sculpture belong to the same formative Kushano-Bactrian period of art as the remarkable finds at Khalchayan, so that, presumably, the material from northern Afghanistan provides yet another link between this belated Hellenistic art in Bactria and the beginnings of Gandhāra art under the Great Kushans.[6]

The relations between ancient Termez and the West in Roman times is supported by an interesting accidental find of a terra-cotta askos (Fig. 19) with a relief of a Dionysian Thiasos closely related to the composition of the Borghese vase [7] and, on the base of the vessel, a zone with various Roman cult objects, bucrania, and bits of armor such as decorate the frieze of the Temple of Vespasian built by Domitian in A.D. 81.[8] This object from the early empire is the Airtam-Termez counterpart of a great many Graeco-Roman objects discovered in the treasure of Begram. Its presence helps to support the theory that, although classical elements in Transoxiana and Gandhāra certainly stem from the Hellenistic art of Bactria, this Western tradition continued to receive new transfusions of Mediterranean styles by contact with the Mediterranean world of the Roman period.

In the now desert and uninhabited region of the lower Amu Darya rise the mountainous ruins of the cities of ancient Chorasmia. This region once formed one of the Eastern satrapies of the Achaemenid Empire before the conquest of Alexander the Great. Although there is some evidence to indicate that these territories were part of the Kushan Empire in the first centuries of our era, it was only after the disintegration of the Indo-Scythian power in the third century A.D. that an indepen-

Fig. 19 – Tonaskos from Termez, U.S.S.R. Hermitage, Leningrad. See above.

dent Chorasmian civilization developed. After a brief moment of flore-scence in the third and fourth centuries, a period of decadence set in during the fifth and sixth centuries and, perhaps owing to a failure in the irrigation systems, the main centers of culture were abandoned in the seventh century, probably even before the Arab invasions. This was a feudal type of culture with noble clans, their retainers and slaves settled in vast fortified manors. Such was the stronghold of Toprak Kala, whose towered battlements enclosed an area 1,900 feet by 1,400 feet. The palace, constructed around a courtyard on a high platform, rose to a height of three stories and was dominated by three gi-gantic towers. It contained three vast halls. The decoration of the so-called Hall of Kings was a combination of stucco sculpture and painting with effigies of the princes of Chorasmia and their families. The Hall of Victories was lined with statues of princes attended by molded figures of Nikes, and the Hall of Warriors was ornamented with reliefs of men-at-arms painted black, perhaps as an indication that Indian mercenaries were in the employ of the lords of Chorasmia. The heads of the rulers preserved in the Hermitage are modeled in stucco covered with a shell of powdered alabaster and polychromy (Ill. 16). As will be seen below, to a far greater degree than the painted effigies of princes at Pyandzhi-kent and Balalik Tepe, these heads give a strong impression of actual

Fig. 20 — Nike. Archaeological Museum, Istanbul. See above.

portraiture, and in this respect are related to the sculpture of Khalchayan
(Ill. 17). These faces have a suggestion of the realism and intensity of
Hellenistic portraits, perhaps an ultimate reflection of the art of Bactria.
With regard to the classical aspect of the sculpture from Toprak Kala
(although the fragmentary statues of Nikes and the draped figure of a
princess [Ill. 11] might be thought of as an inheritance from the Greek
traditions of Bactria or Parthia), considering the late date of this statuary, one cannot help wondering if here as in Gandhāra there were not
fresh contacts with the Roman and Byzantine world. The modeling of
the robe of the princess is not unlike the somewhat formalized revival
of the Hellenistic drapery formula as seen in the fifth-century Byzantine
relief of Nike (Fig. 20). It is of course perfectly legitimate to suppose
that the old Hellenistic style could have survived or been revived in
Khwarezm, just as the same pagan Greek mode survived even in the
Byzantine world. A famous example of direct Byzantine-Hellenistic
workmanship is to be seen in an even later monument, the genii of the
great grotto of Khusrau II (A.D. 590–628). at Taq-i-Bustan.[9] It must

be noted, too, that the universal employment of lime plaster in Chorasmia does not necessarily indicate a borrowing from Gandhāra, since this is a technique that could as easily have found its way to Toprak Kala from contacts with Parthia or early Sasanian Iran.

The last great center of Soghdian civilization was Pyandzhikent, some 70 kilometers east of Samarkand on the plain below the gorges of the Zaravshan River. The great period of artistic florescence of this capital extended from the fifth to the eigth century. We know from Arabic records that the last king of the dynasty, Divashtich, was captured and crucified by the Arabs with the fall of his final stronghold at Mount Mug in 722. This event marked the end of the pre-Islamic culture of ancient Soghdiana.

The capital of Pyandzhikent, a Central-Asian Pompeii, consisted of a fortress, a walled town, or *shahristan,* with innumerable shrines and houses, a suburb and a necropolis. As in so many of the Central Asian kingdoms, the art of Pyandzhikent represents a mixture of so many different styles reflecting contacts with Iran, India, and the classical world, and the strict chronological development of these styles is difficult to establish. As proposed by M. M. Diakonov, the stylistic development of the paintings at Pyandzhikent consists essentially of two manners with minor subdivisions. In the first, and perhaps earlier style, there is an interest in the suggestion of volume and relief with a free and yet delicate handling of the forms.[10] In the second phase, the compositions become practically two-dimensional, linear, and splendidly decorative in effect. Whether this progression is valid or not is difficult to decide. At Pyandzhikent, as at Bāmiyān and Kizil, in determining the chronology of the works one is in danger of falling into the trap of committing the biological fallacy of presupposing a development from the more realistic, solid mode to a more abstract or flat one. The fact of the matter is that, at Pyandzhikent, all we know is that this splendid pageant of Soghdian art came to a fiery end in A.D. 722; and it is quite possible that the different styles represented in the shrines, palaces, and houses of the great city may have been executed more or less contemporaneously by ateliers of artists trained either in an Iranian or Indian tradition, or even, as Diakonov has suggested, in an Armenian or Byzantine milieu.

At Pyandzhikent the subjects of the wall paintings in the shrines and dwellings of the nobility illustrate a vast repertory of epic, mythological, and religious scenes dedicated not to one but to many religions, in cluding Mazdaism, Buddhism, and Manichaeism, as well as purely local cults. This repertory includes such diverse subjects as the Roman wolf,

Episodes from the Legend of Rustam. Wall painting from Room 41, Section VI, Pyandzhikent, Tadzhikistan, USSR. H. 2.5 m. 7th century A.D. *Hermitage, Leningrad.*
The subjects of this specticular mural painting can be specifically related to passages from Firdausi's *Shah-nameh*, the famous epic poem written at Ghazni in the tenth century, based on heroic legends of far earlier periods. The episodes are drawn from the part of the poem entitled *halft-khwan* ("The Seven Stories"). At the left in our illustration, the hero, mounted on a gigantic charger, lassoes the knight Avlod, and at the right, a serpentine dragon, attacked by Rustam, spurts flames from its wounds. This is only a small section of a long painted frieze, which includes many other illustrations of the epic tale. Fragments of a defile of animals may be seen above the upper border of the panel; below were portrayed scenes of ritual and feasting.

the story of the goose that laid the golden egg, a battle of Amazons, and a great frieze dedicated to the epic of Rustam. Still other spectacular painted friezes devoted to Iranian epics have been discovered in recent years but unfortunately remain unpublished.

Many of the episodes in the latter decoration have been specifically related PLATE P. 57 to passages dealing with the exploits of Rustam in Firdausi's *Shah-nameh*. Other verses in this poem, describing the paintings and sculptures of royal palaces, might well apply to the decoration of Pyandzhikent and other Soghdian strongholds. These Rustam stories are part of the world of pre-Islamic Iranian *chansons de geste* and ancient concepts of knightly valor that live on both in Firdausi's poem and in the courtly miniatures of later centuries. The wall paintings of the Rustam legend at Pyandzhikent, like so many others from this famous site, are presumably illustrations of the type of Zoroastrianism that flourished in Western Central Asia.

Mounted Warrior. Fragment of a shield. Wood covered with painted hide. From Mount Mug, Tadzhikistan, USSR. H. 23 cm. Early 8th century A.D. *Hermitage, Leningrad.*
The cavalryman is represented wearing a complete suit of laminated armor, presumably made of strips of hide. He holds a sword or lance over his left shoulder. A long sword hangs down from his belt, and a short mace is strapped to the warrior's waist. What appear to be a bow and quiver are fixed to the back of the "box saddle," quilted with felt with rosette patterns. The horse furniture includes a globelike ornament attached to the bridle over the forehead, and a heavy tassel hangs from the neck. Straps of joined disks around the neck and crupper complete the harness of the steed.

Harpist. Detail of head. Fragment of wall painting from Room 1, Block VI, Pyandzhikent, Tadzhikistan, USSR. H. 132 cm. 7th–8th century A.D. *Hermitage, Leningrad.*
This beautiful fragment of wall painting was removed from a long frieze with adjoining scenes of Mazdean fire worship. The exact significance of the figure is unknown, although, presumably from the presence of the richly decorated nimbus and the hieratic character of the image, it is a portrayal of a deity in the syncretic religious cults that flourished in Pyandzhikent. The very simple harp, seen in our drawing in Fig. 21, resembles instruments of the same type that have survived among the Kafirs in modern times.

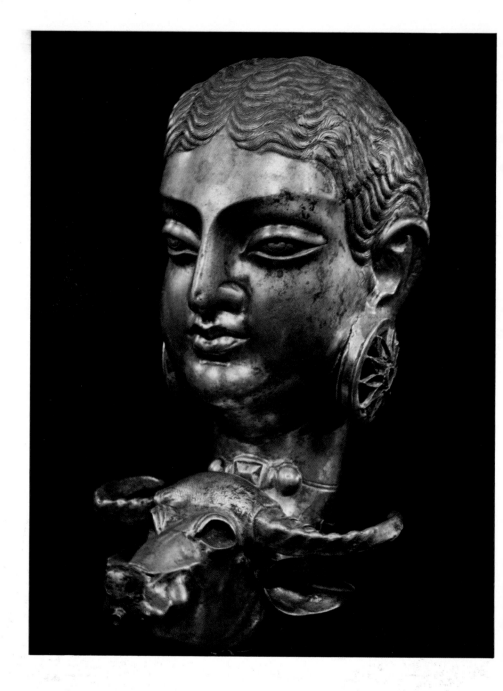

The Angel Drvaspa. Silver rhyton, repoussé and chased and partially gilt. Soghdian. H. 7⅞ in. 5th–7th century A.D. *Cleveland Museum of Art, Cleveland, Ohio.*

The favorite Soghdian device of isolating the principal figures against the flat plane of color reappears in the Rustam frieze. This is a subdivision of Diakonov's "second style." Here the background is a neutralized ultramarine. Although, as in other Soghdian wall paintings, the forms are conceived essentially as flat silhouettes, the overlapping of figures and setting gives a slight illusion of depth. The massive proportions of Rustam's steed cannot fail to remind us of the great warhorses of the Sasanian reliefs at Naqsh-i-Rustam. The pearl border framing the top and bottom of the frieze, as well as traces of the familiar Sasanian roundel on Rustam's mantle, are, of course, reflections of the conventions of Iranian textile design (Figs. 30, 45 and Page 90). Although it is difficult to put into words, we have the feeling in the Rustam cycle that the stylized elegance of drawing, the fanciful and exciting evocation of the world of legend, as well as the delight in color, seem to prophesy that magical transfiguration of reality in Persian miniatures of the Islamic period, just as the *Shahnameh* itself became the great medieval epic of the Iranian people.

The style of this particular cycle at Pyandzhikent appears to be a local and original manner developed in the independent principalities of Turkestan in the last century before the Arabic conquest. The wall painting of figures of horsemen and demons set off against an azure background gives the impression of a gigantic tapestry. There are only slight indications of modeling, and the forms appear as superbly effective silhouettes with an extraordinary delicacy in the entirely linear description of both outlines and interior details.

One of the great treasures of the Hermitage is the female harpist from Pyandzhikent illustrated on Page 58 and in Figure 21. The style of this masterpiece is difficult to define. The figure seems like an adaptation of an Indian Bodhisattva type (cf. Fig. 52) — even to the drawing of the elongated earlobe of Buddhist iconography — and in its svelte attenuation resembles the wooden statues of Pyandzhikent (Ill. 12) and the elongated divinities of Fondukistan (Page 114). The style in its incorporeal elegance and exquisitely refined drawing already anticipates the

The bowl of the vessel, actually the head of the goddess, is soldered to the bull's head, which forms the spout by a collar of silver inside the neck of the two parts of the vessel. It should be noted that, except for the delicate chasing of parts of the rhyton, such as the eyes of the divinity, a few locks of hair, and the stylized hair between the bull's horns, the work was executed entirely in the repoussé technique. The object was found in the Dailaman region of Iran near the southwestern shore of the Caspian.

Fig. 22 – River gods. Stucco frieze from Pendzhikent, U.S.S.R. Hermitage, Leningrad. Compare p. 63.

rarefied ethereal beauty of the painting of Buddhist divinities in Japan of the Fujiwara period. The long thin face with its small delicate features and almond eyes is strangely evocative of the Madonnas of Duccio. Again, the wistful expression of this lovely ethereal mask is a haunting suggestion of such neo-Hellenistic icons as the Vladimirskaya. Once again one is led to conjecture on the problem of the part played by the painting of Pyandzhikent and other Soghdian sites, not only in the formation of later Iranian miniature painting but also the art of Byzantium itself. The style of the painting as a whole, both in the flat linear conception of the form and the color scheme, approximates the mode we have just seen in the frieze of the Rustam legend.

The murals of Pyandzhikent include battle scenes with archers in armor, nobles seated at a ritual meal, and a curious subject, often reproduced, representing two men at a gaming board. The strangely Indian appearance of these personages, one with shoulder flares and the Brahmin chignon, is perhaps an unidentified episode from a Jātaka tale.[11] The attendants at the left of this composition, with their round faces and long eyes, bear a faint resemblance to the types at Balalik Tepe; but beyond such similarities in minor details it is completely impossible to group the paintings of Soghdiana into a single school of art.

The sculptural remains recovered at Pyandzhikent are no less interesting than the wall paintings as revelations of the formation of local styles and the contacts with the artistic and religious traditions of India and Afghanistan.

The nearly life-size statues in carbonized wood, perhaps portraits of warrior princes and princesses, found at Pyandzhikent (Ill. 12), are of extraordinary importance for the origin of certain stylistic elements that spread to other parts of Central Asia. These effigies are extremely attenuated. Some have a sinuous twist of the body suggesting the age-old Indian canon of déhanchement, as seen, for example, in the famous ivory river goddesses of Begram. Both male and female figures are loaded with necklaces, beaded belts, and jewels. The drapery is carved in intricately incised ridges. The suave grace of these statues seems to parallel the Mannerist art of Fondukistan and the eastward spread of this elongated canon to Kashmir and Serindia.

In the iwan of Temple II in the Shahristan sector of Pyandzhikent a long stucco frieze was discovered with representations of tritons, sea monsters, makaras, and fish against a background of conventionalized waves (Fig. 22). This was apparently a dedication to the fructifying powers of water, perhaps an allusion to the water spirits of the Zaravshan itself. Although the snake-legged triton certainly has a family resemblance to the portrayals of these creatures in the sculpture of Mathurā and Gandhāra, in certain details of the frieze, like the figure of a river goddess (Ill. 9), the style of drapery cannot fail to remind us of those belated revivals of Hellenistic art in the Late Antique and Byzantine

Fig. 23 – Ivory diptych of the Symmacher. Victoria and Albert Museum, London. Compare p. 164.

West. It might be compared to such examples of resuscitated Hellenistic art as the figure of a priestess in the famous ivory of the Symmachii in the Victoria and Albert Museum (Fig. 23): in this late fourth century ivory the softly clinging drapery at first seems to bear a striking resemblance to Greek sculpture of the fourth century, but a closer inspection shows a certain dryness and hardness of execution and we are not conscious of any real separation between the substance of the drapery and the body it covers. Both in the last centuries of the Roman world and here in formerly Hellenized Asia, the effort to repeat the ancient classical formula is now a studied technical effort for the artist trying to maintain a vanishing taste and style.

Not only the style of this single figure but the iconography of the entire complex appears related to the so-called "Nāga Porch" recently discovered at Tepe Shotor, Hadda.[12] This extraordinary complex consists of an entire chapel, or porch, dedicated either to the Buddha's encounter with the water spirits or to the worship of the nāgas. The floor is covered with a stucco simulation of the surface of a tank with fish, lotus fronds, and rippling waves. Around the sides of the dry artificial pond appear nāgas in nearly the full round and a number of draped figures, like nereids (Fig. 24), surrounded by sinuous incised lines to suggest the movement of the waves; their soaked draperies, again suggestive of the Late Antique formula seen at Pyandzhikent, are, if anything, like so

Fig. 24 — Nagini. Hadda, Afghanistan. See above.

*Fig. 25 – Distribution of the relics of the Buddha. From Kizil, Chinese Turkestan.
Formerly Berlin. Compare p. 66.*

much of the sculpture of Hadda, even more strongly evocative of the
classical heritage. The site of the Tepe Shotor may be dated in the later
fourth century by the finds of coins of Shapur III (A.D. 383–388).[13]
Whether the river goddess of Pyandzhikent and the nāginis of Hadda are
to be regarded as a last kindling of the Hellenic spirit in Central Asia or
under the direct influence of contemporary Late Antique art is a question that cannot be answered unequivocally. As has been discussed in the
chapter devoted to the art of Gandhāra, it is possible and appropriate to
assume the presence and perhaps enduring influence of the Greek art of
Bactria but, at the same time, it seems certain that Roman influence
continued to affect the art of both Gandhāra and western Central Asia
in the first four centuries of our era.
Mount Mug, located in the wild gorges of the Zaravshan River about
120 kilometers to the east of Pyandzhikent, was the stronghold of the rulers
of Soghdia. As already noted, it was the scene of the capture and crucifixion
of the last king of the region, Divashtich, by the Arabs in A.D. 722. The

Fig. 26 – Clay rhyton from Surkh Kotal, Afghanistan. Compare. p. 70.

PLATE P. 59

excavation of this ruined castle in 1933 brought to light a notable collection of Soghdian texts and also the fragment of a shield that is the subject of our illustration, a pathetic memento of one of the defenders of this last outpost of Soghdian civilization. The horseman wears a variant of the laminated scale armor originally developed by the Romans and Parthians, as seen in many representations of Roman foot soldiers and cavalrymen in the reliefs of the Column of Marcus Aurelius. The appearance of the same type of mail in a wall painting at Kizil provides an argument for the diffusion of Sogdhian styles to innermost Asia (Fig. 25). The massive steed with a balloon-like headdress and straps composed of joined disks around the neck and crupper reminds us of the warhorses of Sasanian rock carvings. As at Pyandzhikent and Afrasiab. the draftsmanship, even on such a piece of military equipment, is extremely free. The drawing of the hands holding the reins and sword gives the same impression of both elegance and tension characteristic of so many examples of painting in the final phase of art in Western Turkestan. It is not difficult to see the figure of the horseman with his attenuated body and wasp waist as a prophecy of the delicate canon perpetuated in Iranian miniatures of the Islamic period in Iran.

A superbly beautiful and interesting metal object, which, as pointed out by Dorothy Shepherd in her original publication of the piece, must be of Soghdian origin, is a silver rhyton in the collection of the Cleveland PLATE P. 60 Museum of Art.[14] The vessel is at once a personification in anthropomorphic and animal form of the angelic Drvaspa, the protectress of flocks and horses. In ancient texts the divinity is described as the soul of the bull and she who keeps horses. This is part of an ancient Iranian iconography, perhaps of ultimate Mesopotamian origin, in which the primordial bull was regarded as the generator of all creatures. The bull's head, in other words, may be a reference to the goddess as the embodiment of the primordial ox or as a reference to one of the beasts under her special protection. We are already aware of the usual form of the rhyton from the Parthian examples at Nisa (Fig. 13), but such an exotic type as the present vessel could only have been made for some very special ritual or sacramental purpose, perhaps for some solemn occasion, investiture, or the ritual feast of Nowruz, the annual spring fertility festival of the Zoroastrian year.

From the stylistic point of view we can recognize the combination of various foreign elements: the full lips and almond eyes and the heavy

Fig. 27 – Envoy from Chaganian. Wall painting. Afrasiab (Samarkand). U.S.S.R. Compare p. 71.

Fig. 28 – Senmurv. Detail from the Chosros II niche, Taq-i-Bustan, Iran. Compare p. 71.

disk earrings may remind us of India. The treatment of the hair is still suggestive of the Hellenistic mode, and the combination of the decorative linear definition of the muscular structure of the bull and the formalization of the planes are familiar Iranian traits.

It is obvious that this rhyton and other objects in precious metal found in the Dailaman region of Iran were not made locally, but found their way to northeastern Iran as tributes or trade from some more easterly center, where elements of Indian, classical, and Iranian origins were combined

Fig. 29 – Senmurv. Detail of a wall painting. Afrasiab (Samarkand), U.S.S.R. Compare p. 71.

68

Ambassadors from Chaganian. Detail of head. Wall painting from Afrasiab (Old Samarkand), Uzbekistan, USSR, 6th–7th century A.D.

The detail in our plate illustrates the head of one of the tribute bearers in the foreground of the composition. The sensitively drawn bearded face appears to be a portrait of a member of the delegation from the small principality of Chaganian. Behind the head, traces of the ultramarine blue background are visible. Portions of the pattern of the robe, boars' heads in medallions, can be seen in the part of the dress shown in the reproduction.

69

Hunter Mounted on an Elephant Fighting Two Leopards. Detail. Wall painting, Red Hall, Varaksha, Uzbekistan, USSR. H. 4ft. 5th–6th century A.D. *Hermitage, Leningrad.*
The illustration shows a section of a long frieze representing a succession of encounters between elephant riders with leopards, tigers, and winged griffins. Above, in a second register, now almost completely destroyed, is a procession of beasts. The hunters and their mahouts at Varaksha are clad in a fanciful combination of Indian and Iranian dress: nude above the waist, they wear skirts or dhotis, a variety of necklaces and armlets, and the typical Iranian ribbons float from their jeweled headdresses. Medallion patterns of Sasanian type ornament the saddlecloth of the rider in our detail. As in other palace buildings in Russion Turkestan, long clay benches or "sofas" extended around the entire perimeter of the room below the painted decorations.

into an original style. Clay rhytons of a somewhat similar type have been found at Afrasiab and Surkh Kotal (Fig. 26). We are already familiar with the wedding of foreign forms and techniques in the Soghdian art of Pyandzhikent. The same fusion of delicate sensuality and refined abstraction appears in the Drvaspa rhyton. Presumably the vessel dates from the fifth or sixth century in the period of the Hephthalite or Turkish domination of the territories of Transoxiana, although, perhaps, the resemblance of the head of the goddess to the Indian types of Fondukistan may make a somewhat later dating preferable.

In its unique iconography and individual style based on the assimilation of foreign forms the rhyton is as characteristic of Soghdian art as the wall paintings and sculpture of Pyandhzikent. Like the beautiful painting of a harpist, the Cleveland Drvaspa has something of the refinement of the sensuous Indian canon in certain heads from Hadda and the inimitable Iranian feeling for elegance of formal design. From the point of view of its sophisticated iconographic and aesthetic aspects, this superb Soghdian object, as will become apparent in the chapter on Afghanistan, is intimately related to the Indo-Iranian style of Fondukistan (cf. Plate p. 114).

The sensational discovery of a cycle of wall paintings, dating from the sixth or seventh century A.D. at Afrasiab, the ancient Samarkand, presents the most spectacular evidence for our knowledge of this Soghdian capital that has come down to us. A Soghdian inscription informs us that this magnificent frieze, some eleven meters in length, represents an ambassador from the small principality of Chaganian to the court of Samarkand. Slightly paraphrased, this remarkable document reads: "When the emissary of the Okhan king, Abarkuhunan, came, he spoke as follows, 'I, the Chagani scribe, son of Bukar, from the Chagani ruler Turanshah... have respectfully come into the presence of the king... And do not have any doubts regarding me and the Samarkand gods. Then at the same time, I am well informed about Samarkand writing, and also of the king's power...'" The composition as a whole, with the figures set off against an azure blue background, represents a defile of envoys, some on horseback, others on camels (Fig. 27). A richly caparisoned elephant, probably the mount of a royal princess, forms part of the procession; in the background, we see a flock of white cranes. Part of the defile is a court lady riding on horseback, an attendant of the bride for the lord of Samarkand or one of his sons. Page 69 illustrates the head of one of the attendants bearing caskets, walking with the slow dignity of Egyptian kings (Ill. 14). The members of the ambassadorial suite are resplendent in magnificent gowns of Sasanian silk, with painted imitations of the patterns of Iranian weavings. The repertory of designs is exceeded only by the carved representations of these Sasanian patterns in the reliefs of Taq-i-Bustan (Fig. 28). Among the typical Sasanian motifs, we note the simurg (Fig. 29), boars' heads, birds bearing beribbonned necklaces, rams, and elephants. The individual beasts and birds, symbolical emblems of the gods of the Mazdean pantheon, are enclosed in pearl medallions. As may be seen in actual examples of Sasanian silk, at the quadrants of each circle is a smaller pearl circlet enclosing a crescent, a device that links each roundel to its neighbors in the patterns (Fig. 30 and 73). The in-

PLATE P. 69

Fig. 30 – Senmurv. Silk fabric. Victoria and Albert Museum, London. Compare p. 71.

dividual animal shapes have the same completely decorative, heraldic character that we shall encounter in other painted replicas of Sasanian designs at Bāmiyān and eastward throughout Serindia.

These faithful imitations of Iranian motifs might at first make us believe that we are dealing with a transplanted Iranian manner, but, in actuality, the style of the Afrasiab murals is quite different from Sasanian monumental figural compositions as we know them in the reliefs of Bishapur and Naqsh-i-Rustam and the fragments of painting discovered by Herzfeld at Kuh-i-Khwaja. Our color plate, and the reproduction in black-and-white, illustrates the extremely free, fluid linear drawing that characterizes the entire mural. Although, in photographs, the Afrasiab cycle may give an impression of greater monumentality in comparison with other wall paintings in Transoxiana, actually the Afrasiab murals are painted with such loving attention to detail — rendered in beautiful colors and with infinitely delicate draftsmanship — that, like a miniature page or such a painting as Gentile da Fabriano's *Epiphany,* they have the effect of drawing the spectator into the picture to explore lovingly every facet of the composition. There is an attempt to suggest the spatial relationship of the members of the suite, not only by the old device of vertical perspective, but also in the very largeness of the forms, in foreshortened poses and three-quarter views. This is a kind of realism quite different from the comparatively decorative styles of Varaksha (Page 70) and Balalik Tepe (Ill. 15). It should be noted, too, that the strongly characterized heads give the impression of portraits rather than generalized types. According to a universal convention in Central Asia, members of different racial types are painted with red or white complexions. We should also note that within the overall impression of monumentally conceived forms moving freely in space, the individual details, in the surely brushed fine lines of the heads and in the portrayal of the intricate patterns of the costumes, are all painted with the greatest delicacy of touch and refinement. Although I have no intention of suggesting a counterinfluence from the East, the Arasiab wall paintings give the same impression of figures in space represented essentially in linear terms that we find in related processional subjects in Chinese painting of the Six Dynasties and T'ang periods.

In the desert regions some 20 miles west of Bokhara lies Varaksha, the capital of the pre-Islamic rulers of the Bokhara oasis. The citadel and palace were built of the same sun-dried bricks (*paksha*) which are employed for the construction of fortified manors in Afghanistan today. The most interesting discoveries at this site were the sculptured and painted decorations of the castle. These are believed to date from the sixth century, when the palace was reconstructed. The most striking decorations were found in the Red Hall of the palace in a wall painting representing a fantastic hunting scene. Princely personages with *kusti* or hair ribbons streaming from their diadems are shown mounted on PLATE P. 70 diminutive elephants engaged in combat with rearing leopards, tigers, and winged griffins. Unlike some of the cycles of Pyandzhikent, these scenes at Varaksha are not taken from an epic, but, like the combats of the king of kings with various monsters carved at Persepolis, appear to be painted as a symbolic and ebulliently decorative reference to the invincible prowess of the sovereign and his lords.

The dramatic silhouettes of men and beasts set off against a Pompeiian red background give the impression of a vast tapestry girdling the chamber. This decorative effect is enhanced by the manner in which the forms are presented in terms of line and flat tone. The entire composition is two-dimensional and, although filled with action, the scenes of the hunters and the hunted have a frozen, heraldic quality reminiscent of

73

Sasanian art: the combatants appear to be petrified in a moment of violent movement, like the symbolic representations of jousting horsemen in the rock carvings of Naqsh-i-Rustam. It is possible to find other similarities to Sasanian forms in metalwork and textiles and in certain Iranian details of costume, such as the long fluttering hair-ribbons. It may be noted, too, that, as at Pyandzhikent, the two zones of the painting are separated by a pearl border; certain details, like the griffin's wing with its long spiraling feathers divided by a jeweled band, are familiar conventions in the portrayal of the simurg and other fabulous creatures in the repertory of Sasanian silk weaving. Although the Varaksha wall paintings are marked by the same predilection for the patternized treatment of forms that we have observed at Pyandzhikent, they exhibit a far greater concern for decoration for its own sake.

The connection with Iranian art is notable in another apartment of the palace, the East Room, where we find a meticulous representation of Sasanian silk designs, such as the motif of the bird holding a pearl necklace (Fig. 43), which, as we shall see, also appears in the similar painted imitations of fabrics at Bāmiyān and other sites on the northern Silk Road. Whereas the hunting frieze in the Red Chamber is a purely secular painting, representations of worship before a fire altar certainly indicate the presence of a Mazdean cult. Perhaps, in conclusion, the Varaksha murals in their bold, magnificent designs may be best described as only one of many autonomous local styles that emerged in the regions beyond the eastern frontiers of Iran in the Sasanian period.

The excavation of the castle of Varaksha also unearthed a great mass of stucco decorations, which it is believed originally formed a zone of relief above the painted zone of the wall. Although it was impossible to reconstruct the original composition of this frieze, the repertory of subjects includes animal forms, human figures (Ill. 20), and fragments of sirenlike feathered creatures. Although superficially the technique, and especially the beast motifs, suggests the lime-plaster décor of Sasanian Iran as seen at Ctesiphon and Damghan, the treatment of the material is totally different at Varaksha. As may be seen especially well in the human heads from this site, the execution is extremely sketchy, the artist working *au premier coup* with a few strokes of a knife or stick to produce an effect of extraordinary expressiveness. As Professor Belenitskii has pointed out, this plastic understatement is totally different from the rather dryly molded Sasanian plasterwork and the detailed, finished surface treatment of the stucco technique as we know it at Hadda and Toprak Kala. The excavation of Balalik Tepe located in the Surkhan Darya district in southeastern Uzbekistan revealed the remains of a small fortified manor that was the seat of a princely Hephthalite clan. One of the larger rooms was decorated with a painted frieze representing a ritual banquet (Ill. 15). This part of the palace was never restored when the castle was partially rebuilt after the Turkish conquest of this region in A.D. 567. As at Varaksha, the decoration consisted of a long band of painting extending around all four walls of the apartment. The subject is a feast, perhaps the celebration of Nowruz, with men and women seated or reclining on low cushions. They are wearing magnificent mantles faced with silk fabric of an unmistakable Sasanian appearance. The guests hold carinated stemmed cups and mirrors. Behind them, against an azure background, are fan-bearing attendants in a smaller scale. The patterns on the garments represent a great variety of motifs, originating in Sasanian designs, although the representations of boars' heads in roundels are not segmented by either small pearl rings or square-cut jewels. The countenances of the members of this assemblage of courtiers are all of a uniform type, with round faces, large eyes, and small mouths, perhaps a conventional representation of a racial type not dissimilar to the faces of the Uzbeks and the Tadzhiks of today.

Although certain features of the style of Balalik Tepe, such as the massively proportioned figures presented with the flatness of textural design, and their static ritual gestures, are all reminiscent of Sasanian forms, what we see here is just as individual a manner as that of the cycle at Varaksha. There is no suggestion of any spatial depth in the way in which these two-dimensional figures are shuffled, one overlapping the other, like so many court cards, and together with precise wirelike draftsmanship, appear to present us with a manner special to this oasis. A notable compositional device at Balalik Tepe is the placing of the completely two-dimensional figures in overlapping zones to create a symbolical rather than a real space. This aspect of the Balalik style and certain elements of form and technique, as will be noted later, seem to bear some relationship to Bāmiyān, but only to the extent that one would expect from exchanges between these various local art centers, which were perhaps served by itinerant bands of painters on the periphery of the Iranian world.

As will have been noted, all of the works of art from Russian Central Asia described in the preceding paragraphs are either devoted to Mazdean and other local cults or are secular and decorative in character. This brings us to the important subject of Buddhist art in these same Transoxian realms.

The vast eroded ramparts of ancient Merv, rising more like natural formations or giant dunes in the desert solitude of Margiana (Turkmenistan), encompass a number of vanished cities notably the Antiochiae Margiana of the Seleucid period, known to modern archaeologists as Giaur-Kala. Among the many fascinating discoveries by G. A. Koshelenko made in the innermost fastness of this citadel was a large stupa built of clay blocks painted red and, in plan and elevation, closely resembling the arrangement of Buddhist relic mounds in Afghanistan and Gandhāra. Finds of coins of the Sasanian kings Shapur I (A.D. 241–273) and Shapur II (A.D. 279–309) appear to fix the date of this monument in the third and fourth centuries A.D. It has been conjectured that the anti-Buddhist propaganda of Varahran II's adviser, Kartir, the Mazdean evangelist of the late third century, put an end to the completion of the structure. The single most important discovery at this site was that of the head of a colossal Buddha image, measuring 75 centimeters in height, fashioned out of clay with reeds as a binding medium and covered with a layer of powdered alabaster as a base for the polychromy (Fig. 31). The separate snail-shell curls, painted blue, as in a similar head found at Adzhina Tepe, were separately molded and attached to the head (Fig. 32). Even in its fragmentary condition it is not difficult to see the resemblance of this fragment to Buddhist stucco heads from Hadda and other sites in Gandhāra (Fig. 33). The Kushan coins of the second century A.D. provide a terminus ante quem for this Buddhist foundation and for the extension of Kushan influence into Margiana, just as the stupa and the colossal head are the first archaeological evidence we have for the penetration of Buddhism into the realm of the Parthians and Sasanians: we have already noted the missions of the Parthian Buddhist teachers, An Shih-kāo and An Hsüan, to China in the second century A.D.

One of the most important archaeological undertakings in Russian Turkestan has been the excavation of Adzhina Tepe in the Vakhsh Valley (Tadzhikistan), carried on since 1960 by B. A. Litvinskii and T. I. Zeymal. The excavators have brought to light the remains of a Buddhist monastery and an adjoining temple structure. Like their counterparts in Afghanistan and in Transoxiana, the buildings of Adzhina Tepe were made of large unbaked clay blocks. As the discoverer, B. A. Litvinskii, has pointed out, one of the most significant architectural features of Adzhina Tepe is the construction of the monastery with four vaulted iwans which open into the central courtyard and appear to anticipate the plans of the madrasa of the Islamic period. For our present interests the most significant part of the excavations consists of the extraordinary sculptural decorations. More than 500 fragments of statuary were found in the

Fig. 31 — *Head of a colossal statue of the Buddha. From Merv, U.S.S.R. Compare p. 76.*
Fig. 32 — *Head of the Buddha, from Adzhina Tepe, U.S.S.R. Dushanbe Museum. Compare p. 76.*
Fig. 33 — *Head of the Buddha, from Fondukistan, Afghanistan. Kabul Museum. Compare p. 76.*

ruined structure. Following the universal technique of plastic decoration in Western Turkestan, both the devotional figures and reliefs were fashioned from painted clay. According to the reports from the excavators, abundant coin finds make it possible to date the entire complex in the seventh and early eighth centuries A.D.; that is, on the eve of the Arab onslaught on Central Asia. As will become apparent, this positive numismatic dating is of supreme importance for the chronology of related works both north and south of the Oxus in the last centuries of Buddhist art in western Central Asia. One of the most spectacular finds in Adzhina Tepe was a gigantic statue of Buddha in Nirvāna, some 12 meters in length (Fig. 47). The treatment of the robe with the highly conventionalized folds represented by parallel stringlike ridges appears like an echo of the style of the 53-meter Buddha at Bāmiyān in Afghanistan, which is discussed in a later chapter.

A single detail that differentiates this image from the typical conventionalization of late Buddhist statuary in Afghanistan and Gandhāra is the extraordinary naturalism of the enormous hand of Śākyamuni relaxed in death. It is precisely this feeling for a kind of mannered realism within an essentially hieratic formula that, as will be seen, relates the Adzhina sculptures to the last phase of Buddhist art in Afghanistan. In the same way the heads of Buddha unearthed at Adzhina Tepe (Fig. 32), modeled in the formula that is a combination of the classical ideality of

Gandhāra and the fullness of Indian art of the Gupta period, are stylistically very close to the painted clay Buddhas of Fondukistan (Fig. 33). This relationship also pertains to the Bodhisattva torsos discovered at Adzhina. Their presence of course points to the penetration of Mahāyāna concepts to Tadzhikistan in the seventh century. One notable fragment (Ill. 13) in the soft Indian treatment of the torso and clinging drapery is extremely close in style to the supremely beautiful images found at Fondukistan, as will be seen in the next chapter.

1. R. Ghirshman, *Persian Art, The Parthian Sasanian Dynasties, 249* B.C.–A.D. *651,* New York, 1962. Figs. 196–220.
2. Ghirshman, *op. cit.,* Fig. 49.
3. Sir Mortimer Wheeler, *Flames over Persepolis,* New York, 1968, pp. 71–77.
4. *Ibid.,* pp. 83 and 85.
5. Bernard, P., "Deuxième campagne de fouilles d'Aï Khanoum en Bactriane," *CRAI,* April–June, 1967, pp. 317–318.
6. In a recent article the Japanese professor Takayasu Higuchi has proposed the designation "Oxus School of Buddhist Art" (*Bukkyō Geijutsu,* vol. VI, July 1969).
7. M. Bieber, *The Sculpture of the Hellenistic Age,* New York, 1955, p. 166.
8. Curtius-Nawrath, *Das Antike Rom,* Vienna-Munich, 1944, Taf. 10.
9. F. Sarre, *Die Kunst des Alten Persien,* Berlin, 1922, Taf. 91.
10. Tamara Talbot Rice, *Ancient Arts of Central Asia,* New York, 1965, Flg. 86.
11. Talbot Rice, *op. cit.,* Fig. 88.
12. M. and S. Mostamindi, "Nouvelles fouilles à Hadda (1966–1967) par l'Institut Afghan d'Archéologie," *Arts Asiatiques,* XIX, 1969, pp. 15–36.
13. Mostamindi, *op. cit.,* p. 23.
14. D. G. Shepherd, "Two Silver Rhyte," *The Bulletin of the Cleveland Museum of Art,* Oct. 1966, pp. 289–317.

V. AFGHANISTAN

THE CROSSROADS OF ASIA

Afghanistan, at the convergence of the arterial network of roads joining East and West in the ancient period, can be described as in every way the heart of Asia, enclosed by the territories of Iran, Transoxiana, India, and the deserts of Sinkiang. In the period of Buddhist supremacy from the advent of the Kushans until the Arab conquests of the eighth century we may regard Afghanistan as the recipient of various influences from all corners of the world and the spawning ground for techniques and styles that were to affect the artistic destinies of all surrounding realms. Afghanistan could be described as a beautiful and savage landscape with fertile plains along the river valleys and vast desert areas, all locked within the walls of the highest mountains in Asia — the Hindu Kush, the Pamirs, and along the southern border, the spurs of the Himalayas.

We have already described the remnants of Graeco-Bactrian culture in Afghanistan as represented by the finds at Ay Khanum and the medals of the Bactrian kings. What concerns us now is the rise of Buddhist art in this same strategic region. As we have seen, the earliest Buddhist art in Afghanistan is really an extension of the school of Gandhāra. To this phase belongs the stone and stucco sculpture of Hadda and the later schist carvings from Pāitāvā and Shotorak, monastic sanctuaries near the ancient Kushan capital, Kāpiśa (Begram). The real florescence of Buddhism and its art took place north of the Kabul Valley in the Hindu Kush region and as far north as the Amu Darya. These sites in northern Afghanistan, or Afghan Turkestan, are unquestionably products of the period following the disintegration of the Great Kushan dynasty in the mid-third century when these territories came under the control of the Sasanians and, later, of their vassals the Hephthalites.

Although it is customary and convenient to select the Shibar Pass as the continental divide between the basins of the Indus and the Oxus, the Indian and Central Asian worlds, it must be borne in mind that art cannot be compartmented entirely by such geographical barriers. For example, Fondukistan, located in the Ghorband Valley below the Shibar Pass, is in the sphere of Central Asian art. Bāmiyān, Surkh Kotal, and Bactria are related to the sites north of the Oxus; the terrain of the

Kabul Valley southward to the Khyber Pass lies within the orbit of the art of Gandhāra and India.

At least a passing reference must be made at this point to the famous site of Surkh Kotal on the road to Bactria north of the Hindu Kush. This Kushan acropolis built around a lofty eminence was, like the royal shrine of Mat at Mathurā, a sanctuary dedicated to the divine kingship of the rulers of the first Kushan dynasty. A long inscription in the Kushan language, but carved with Greek letters, proclaims a dedication in the reign of the great Kanishka. Flanking the cella at the summit of the great staircase of this Kushan acropolis were found fragmentary statues of the Kushan rulers, two of them dressed in the great mantle and felt boots (Fig. 34) that we see in the famous portrait of Kanishka from Mat (Fig. 35). These and a third image representing a princely personage in a long, bejeweled *pustin* were the objects of a cult of divinized royalty, like their famous counterparts at Nimrud Dagh and Parthian Hatra.[1] Also erected on this citadel of the Kushanshahr was a fire temple closely resembling the plans of similar sanctuaries of the sacred element of Ahura Mazda in Parthian and Sasanian Iran. The presence of this Mazdean shrine only reinforces our idea of the syncretic nature of the Kushan religion, implied by the great pantheon of Greek, Iranian, Hindu, and Buddhist deities that appear on the coinage of Kanishka and Huvishka.[2]

Fig. 34 – Statue of Kanishka from Surkh Kotal, Afghanistan. Kabul Museum. Compare p. 81.

Fig. 35 – Statue of Kanishka. Archaeological Museum, Muttra. Compare p. 81.

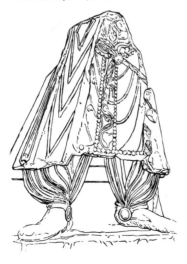

I have always been of the opinion that royal portrait sculpture at Surkh Kotal, in its hieratic frontality and formalism derived from Parthian prototypes, like the effigies of W'ima Kadphises and Kanishka at Mathurā, represents a style special to the Kushans. This sculpture dedicated to the cult of the great Kushan sovereigns has been described by Professor John Rosenfield as the dynastic art of the Kushans. These fragmentary imperial likenesses, together with a number of heads from the royal shrine of Mat at Mathurā, appear to stand apart from both the traditions of India and Gandhāra. All of these dynastic cult images are characterized by their rigid frontality and a ceremonial idol-like quality intended to command awe and respect (Figs. 34 and 35). More attention is paid to the rendering of the Kushan costume and the attributes of might than the suggestion of a physical presence: in these statues, the "body" appears to be simply an armature to support the heavy, sometimes be-jeweled, mantles and the sword and mace of imperial power. This hieratic character and the emphasis on splendid details of costume relate this special category of Kushan sculpture to the similar royal portrait sculpture of Parthia, as exemplified in the famous bronze statue of a prince from Shami and the royal portraits of Hatra. The Kushan portrait statues are just as original and separate a form of artistic expression as the work of the autonomous communities of artists who served the ancient principalities of Chorasmia and Soghdiana. As has already been observed, the finding of a plaque at Khalchayan presumably representing an enthroned Kushan ruler (Fig. 15), resembling the famous image of W'ima Kadphises at Mathurā (Fig. 16), appears to indicate that this mode of portraying divinized rulers had its beginnings in the first century A.D. when the Indo-Scythians were established in the Transoxian regions of ancient Bactria. The presence of this Kushan art at the gates of Central Asia provides one more stylistic ingredient that went into the formation of the art of Serindia and perhaps Transoxiana as well. Lastly, the different divinities — classical Mazdean, Hindu, and Buddhist — which appear on the coins of the early Kushan rulers, give us some idea of the diversity of beliefs that flourished in the Kushanshahr; as we have already encountered a similar catholicity of cults in the principalities of Western Turkestan.

In this connection, a slight historical digression is necessary in order to explain the art that appeared in Afghan Turkestan in the centuries after the fall of the great Kushan dynasty.

Following the invasion of Shapur I in 241, a raid, which, according to some scholars, extended as far as Peshawar, the power of the Kushans was limited to Gandhāra and the Punjab. The appearance of names like Vasudeva among the later rulers suggests the gradual Indianization of the originally Scythian dynasty. The situation becomes more confused in the fourth century when eastern Afghanistan and the lands south of the Hindu Kush fell into the hands of a tribe known as the Kidara, or Kidara Kushans. Probably both the Kidaras and another group, known as the Chionites, in the former portions of the Kushan Empire north of the Oxus, were under Sasanian influence. By the middle of the fifth century the history of these regions becomes more involved with the appearance of the Hephthalites, sometimes characterized as Huns, although in actuality they may have been part of the tribal complex including the Chionites and Kidaras. The empire of the Hephthalites was centered in eastern Iran, and their conquest of Afghanistan and parts of northern India are known from Indian sources. Throughout the fifth century, Sasanian armies were repeatedly defeated by the Hephthalites: the Emperor Peroz died in battle against them in 484. It was only in A.D. 558 that an alliance between the Sasanians and the Western Turks was able to crush the Hephthalite power. Thereafter, the Sasanians enjoyed a sovereignty over the former Hephthalite principalities south of the Oxus and probably in the Hindu Kush region as well. It was precisely in these territories that some of the most notable monuments for the later Buddhist art of Afghan Turkestan are found.

The most important center of Buddhism and its art in Afghan Turkestan was at Bāmiyān, some 240 kilometers northwest of Kabul. Bāmiyān lies at the intersection of important roads — the highways leading southward from Herat and Balkh and Transoxiana; another route, branching off at Shahr-i-Zohak, crosses the Unai Pass to the Kabul Valley on the way to India. The main approach to the East leads over the Shibar Pass and through the defiles of the Ghorband Valley to emerge into the plain of the Panjir and Kabul rivers at Charikar, near the ancient capital of Kapiśa (Begram), from where other trails lead at last to the Pamirs and the road to Serindia and Cathay. It has been conjectured that the appearance of Hecate, goddess of the crossroads, on the coins of the Bactrian king, Demetreus II, may be a reference to Bāmiyān and its position in the days of Alexander's successors. It was precisely this strategic location that makes Bāmiyān and its art a kind of roundabout for the reception and diffusion of art forms from the classical, Iranian, and Indian worlds.

Bāmiyān is mentioned in the travel diary of Hsüan-tsang in the seventh century as a stronghold of the Lokottaravadins, a proto-Mahāyāna sect, and Huei-ch'ao in 827 describes the convent as a center of Mahāyāna. There are references to this famous site by the Arabic chroniclers Tabari and Yakut. The end came for this romantic site and its civilization in 1222, when Genghis Khan in revenge for the death of his son beneath the walls of Shahr-i-Zohak, methodically slaughtered every man, woman, and child, and every bird and beast in the valley. Then, all was silence, until the eighteenth century, when the Mogul Emperor Aurengzeb fractured the legs of the colossal Buddha with his fieldpieces. The pioneer archaeologist Charles Masson and Lieutenant Burnes visited the desolate valley before 1840. We have descriptions and sketches of the caves by Lady Sale and Lieutenant Eyre who were among the British prisoners sequestered at Bāmiyān after the disaster of the Jagdalik Pass in the Afghan War of 1840. The credit for the scientific investigation and restoration of this famous Buddhist monument belongs to the pioneers of the French Archaeological Mission in Afghanistan: Godard, Hackin, and Carl.

The valley of Bāmiyān, set between the towering peaks of the Hindu Kush and the Koh-i-Baba ranges, is one of the most beautiful and spectacular sites in Afghan Central Asia. The approach to the capital that once existed there was guarded by the great citadel of Shahr-i-Zohak, set on a natural platform atop a sheer red cliff some miles to the east of Bāmiyān proper. Before its complete devastation by Genghis Khan, the city of Bāmiyān covered the hill of Shahr-i-Gholgola and probably parts of the valley floor, like the modern village huddled at the floor of the sheer cliff of conglomerate stone that rises on the northern side of the valley overlooking the Bāmiyān River bordered by green fields and thickets of chunar trees. For several miles the face of this escarpment is honeycombed with scores of rock-cut grottoes, hollowed from the stone to serve as assembly halls, chapels, and sanctuaries for one of the greatest Buddhist monastic communities in all Central Asia (Ill. 21).

The principal caves stretch for about a mile between two gigantic Buddha images set in niches at the eastern and western ends of the complex. At the west stands the 53 meter Buddha, still the largest statue in the world; and forming the focal point of another complex of convent cells at the eastern end of the cliff was enshrined a smaller icon rising to a height of 35 meters. Hsüan-tsang, the famous Chinese pilgrim of the seventh century, describes these colossi in his account of Bāmiyān:

> To the northeast of the royal city there is a mountain, on the declivity of which is placed a stone figure of Buddha, erect, in height 140 or 150 feet. Its golden hues sparkle on every side, and its precious ornaments dazzle the eyes by their brightness . . . To the

east ... there is a standing figure of Sākya Buddha ... in height 100 feet (Ill. 22).

Yakut, who began his famous geographical dictionary in 1218, left us the following awesome description of Bāmiyān, written on the eve of the Mongol conquest:

> There one sees a structure of an elevation prodigious in height; it is supported by gigantic pillars [3] and covered with paintings of all the birds created by God. In the interior are two immense idols carved in the rock and rising from the foot of the mountain to the summit ... One cannot see anything comparable to these statues in the whole world.

The smaller Buddha Śākyamuni is sheltered in a parabolic niche, at one time covered completely with wall paintings. This towering vaulted recess seems like an adaptation of the iwan, the typical arched opening of Sasanian palaces, also incorporated in the buildings at Varaksha and Adzhina Tepe. The statue itself consists of a core of roughly shaped rock, covered with a thick layer of clay with a binding medium of straw for the modeling of the drapery and features. This clay shell was coated with a final layer of lime plaster and originally covered with brilliant polychromy. The style of this statue with its voluminous folds of drapery revealing the form of the body beneath is an enormous enlargement in the classical manner of the Buddha images of Gandhāra (Ill. 1). The robe

Fig. 36 – Sun god. Wall painting in the niche of the 35-meter-high Buddha, Bamiyan, Afghanistan. Compare p. 85.

is an accommodation of the drapery of the toga in the images of Imperial Rome to the Buddha's mantle, or *sanghāti*. This image, judging from the still strongly classical style of the garment, might have been executed as early as the second or third century A.D., certainly much earlier than the completely Sasanian cycle of wall paintings decorating the sides and vault of the niche. Such an early dating for this image may seem hazardous, especially in view of what we shall discover about the indisputable chronology of the wall paintings of the whole complex surrounding the 35-meter image: for these a date no earlier than the late sixth or early seventh century is imperative. The only conclusion possible is that the murals were added some centuries after the completion of the colossus, or that, even though the style of the giant statue reminds us of the early, more classical type of Gandhāra Buddha images, there are many examples of the survival or revival of the early Gandhāra manner in more easterly Central Asian sites, such as Khotan, Kizil, and Shorchuk, all datable between the fourth and eighth centuries. Although it has been suggested that the wall paintings at Bāmiyān were continually renewed over a period of centuries, the very consistency of the Iranian architectural, sculptural, and pictorial decoration of the whole complex of caves centered on the 35-meter Buddha strongly suggested that these decorations were planned and carried out once and for all at the same time.

From the iconographical point of view, the purpose of such a gigantic image, as in classical antiquity, notably in the huge portraits of the Emperor Constantine, was to indicate the more than mortal stature of the personage portrayed; in this case, to present the Buddha as a veritable Mahāpurusa or embodiment of the cosmos. It is important to repeat in this connection Hsüan-tsang's statement that the community at Bāmiyān belonged to the Lokottaravadin sect, in which, as a transition to fully developed Mahāyāna doctrine, the supernatural nature of the Buddha was recognized.

All of the painted decorations in the niche of the 35-meter Buddha and in the various chapels and assembly halls joined to it by stairways and corridors hewn within the cliff are done in what may be described as a provincial version of the style of Iranian art of the Sasanian period.[4] This entire cycle of murals must have been painted when Bāmiyān and large parts of Afghanistan were under Sasanian rule or, as has already been noted, when these territories were controlled by the Hephthalites as the vassals of the last Sasanian monarchs.

One of the largest surviving wall paintings at Bāmiyān is the decoration of the soffit of the niche, a representation of a solar deity in his chariot   PLATE P. 87

Fig. 37 – Surya. Relief from a
stone fence. Bodh Gaya, India.
Compare p. 88.

(Fig. 36). The god himself is clad in a flaring mantle with wide lapels
and a long straight sword attached to the belt, a costume that resembles
the cloak of the effigy of King Kanishka at Mathurā and finds its way
into the dress of noble personages at Kizil and other sites in Eastern
Turkestan. The divinity stands in a toothed halo, a type of aureole found
in portrayals of Helios and other solar gods in the Late Antique Mediterranean world. On the chariot ride the Dawn Maidens, companions of

As may be seen in the drawing, Figure 36, this immense composition represents a divinity dressed in
a long mantle, standing in a quadriga drawn by winged horses. On the celestial car to the right and
left of the deity are helmeted and winged female figures holding spears and shields. They are
probably to be identified as the Dawn Maidens, companions of the Indian sun-god Sūrya. Above
these figures are human-headed birds, or *kinnaras*, and over the head of the sun-god, personifications
of the winds, holding billowing scarves over their heads, and flying geese, or *hainsa*. The composition
as a whole resembles representations of Sūrya, although the inclusion of the *kinnaras* and wind gods
presents a symbolical vision of the entire celestial sphere. Our detail of the mural shows one of the
Dawn Maidens and the remnants of the white steeds with crimson wings. At the left may be seen
an irregular ruddy enframement, an abstract suggestion of clouds, which at one time surrounded the
entire composition. Whether this is a representation of Sūrya or the Iranian Mithra is unimportant,
since in either case we appear to have a symbolical reference to the solar character of the Buddha
often referred to in early texts.

A Sun-god in his Chariot. Detail. Wall painting on the soffit of the niche of the 35-m. Buddha, Bāmiyān, Afghanistan. 6th–7th century A.D.

Buddha and Donors. East wall at the summit of the niche of the 35-m. Buddha, Bāmiyān, Afghanistan. 6th–7th century A.D.
The detail of this wall painting, just below the portrayal of the solar divinity, shows a Buddha flanked by the figure of a disciple, or arhat, and to the right one of a number of donors. The Buddha's attendants are represented as though seated behind a balustrade decked with a textile hanging. The globelike crown of the princely donor has parallels in Sasanian coin portraits. Both this donor and the Buddha at the left are adorned with hair ribbons or *kusti*, again borrowed from the royal Sasanian regalia.

Sūrya in Indian as in the well-known reliefs at Bodh Gayā (Fig. 37) and Bhājā. The winged horses of the quadriga are deployed to the right and left of the tongue of the chariot.

It would not be unlikely to suppose in the syncretic combination of Iranian and Indian elements, both stylistic and iconographic, that the sun god portrayed may be Mithra, and his winged companions, Bamya and Usah, the handmaids of the dawn. There are vague reminiscences of the

Medallion with representation of a boar's head. Diam. ca. 38 cm. Fragment of wall painting from the ceiling of the vestibule of Group D, Bāmiyān, Afghanistan. 6th–7th century A.D. *Kabul Museum.* This fragment is a part of a decoration originally covering the entire ceiling of the narthex of one of the sanctuaries adjoining the niche of the 35-m. Buddha. It is a painted imitation of a familiar Sasanian textile design. The boar's head, which appears in similar painted replicas of textiles at Balalik Tepe and Afrasiab in Russian Turkestan, is a symbol of the Mazdean god of victory Verethragna. This division of the circle of pearls by jewel shapes appears to be typical of Sasanian-style silks woven in Central Asia and may be seen in a crude Chinese imitation found at Astana (Turfan), dated A.D. 661–665 (Fig. 44).

so-called Athena of the Lahore Museum [5] and a helmeted figure identified as Athena at Khalchayan.[6] Visible above the winged goddess in our reproduction is a creature, half human, half bird, probably to be identified as one of the sirens who in planetary mythology controlled the music of the spheres. The sky symbolism of the whole composition is completed

Boar's head in medallion. Silk textile (weft twill) from Astana, Turfan, Chinese Turkestan. Diam. 23.5 cm., H. 24.5 cm. 6th–7th century A.D. *Stein Collection, National Museum, New Delhi.*

"The Blue Bodhisattva." Wall painting on the soffit of the niche of Group E, Bāmiyān, Afghanistan. 6th–7th century A.D.

The painting portrays a Bodhisattva, probably Maitreya, the right hand raised in the *vitarka mudrā*. A rainbow arc appears to support the figure, which was painted on the vault above a now ruined figure of the Buddha. Framing the divinities are slender colonnettes surmounted by formalized Corinthian capitals. These in turn support truncated triangles enclosing figures of arhats. The style is a combination of elements of Iranian, Gandhāran, and Indian origin that seems to mark the first appearance of a Central Asian style which reached its final development in the wall paintings of Kizil in the Kucha oasis.

This fragment, like many others found in the cemetery at Astana, was used to cover the face of the dead. The design is the same abstract and symbolical personification of Verethragna seen in the painted imitation of a textile from Group D at Bāmiyān. It will be noted that in the present example the circle is divided at the quadrants not by the square-cut jewel shapes seen in the wall painting, but by smaller circles of pearls enclosing crescents. This device linked the medallion to the adjoining roundels in the woven fabric. It is found in rare fragments of actual Sasanian textiles, such as the simurg in the Victoria and Albert Museum (Fig. 30), as well as in early silk fragments from Antinoë in Egypt, but presumably woven in Iran proper.

91

Colossal Buddha. Conglomerate stone, covered with clay and stucco and originally painted. H. 53 m. 5th–7th century A.D. Bāmiyān, Afghanistan.

at the summit of the painting by the figures of wind gods with fluttering scarves, and the flying geese, or hamsa, sometimes interpreted as souls received into the highest heaven. The sun god and his train are shown as though emerging from banks of fiery clouds framing the sides of the composition, so that, even though the forms themselves are flatly painted, the picture gives something of the special illusion of a Baroque ceiling decoration.

The whole composition is, as in many examples of early Indian art, a symbolic reference to the Buddha as an embodiment of cosmic forces, in this case, the sun god. Taken in conjunction with the Seven Buddhas of the Past and Maitreya, who appear on each side of the ceiling composition on the haunch of the vault, the entire arrangement could refer symbolically to the birth of Sākyamuni, as the texts relate, like his predecessors in earlier aeons, arising as another sun to illuminate the darkness of the world. This iconography involving the Buddhas of the past is essentially a Hinayāna concept, but the enormous size of the statue of Sākyamuni already suggests the inception of the Mahāyāna ideal of the Buddha as a cosmic being.

Painted around the haunches of the vault directly below the solar deity are the Seven Buddhas of the Past and Maitreya, separated by figures of donors. The Buddhas are shown seated frontally; the attendants, generally in three-quarter view, appear as half figures behind a rail hung with carpets or patterned cloth. These donors or devotees present a perfect illustration of the adaptation of the Sasanian style to Buddhist usage: they have the massive proportions and inert bulk of Sasanian rock carv-

PLATE P. 88

The giant image of Buddha is housed in a cusped niche, the walls and vault of which were at one time completely covered with wall paintings. The face of the image above the mouth has been destroyed at the top of the niche have suffered the same fate. Our illustration reveals the technique employed for the molding of the drapery on the stone core. The body and head of the statue were roughly hewn from the pudding stone of the cliff. As in the case of the 35-m. Buddha at Bāmiyān this armature supported a thick shell of clay covered with an outer layer of stucco as a base for the final polychromatic decoration. As may be seen in our plate, the drapery was affixed by an ingenious method whereby wooden dowels were driven into the stone surface and joined by cords over which the individual folds of the garment were molded.

Iconographically the giant statue is certainly intended as a representation of the Universal Buddha, perhaps Vairocana, and the countless painted representations of Buddhas, Bodhisattvas, and adoring divinities that once covered the whole interior of the niche are the myriad emanations of the Cosmic Buddha in what becomes thereby a kind of plastic and pictorial mandala. If Lieutenant Burnes's curious statement, made at the time of his visit to Bāmiyān in 1832, that "there appears to have been a tiara on the head" is to be accepted, the identification of the giant Buddha as the Lord of the Universe, or indeed as Vairocana, would be even more convincing. It will be recalled that in his account of Bāmiyān written in the the seventh century, Hsüan-tsang refers to the 53-m. statue as a Buddha whereas the smaller 35-m. image is specifically identified as Sākyamuni.

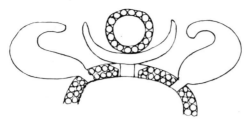

ings and are reminiscent, too, of slight overlapping of two zones of essentially flat forms and of the somewhat more refined quasi-Iranian style of the paintings of the noble assemblage at Balalik Tepe (Ill. 15).

It will be remembered from our short account of the post-Kushan history of Afghanistan that, during the reign of the last great Sasanian king, Khusrau II (A.D. 590–628), the presumably Hephthalite princes of the territories of northern and central Afghanistan were vassals of the Sasanian throne. The coins of Śrī Vasudeva (Fig. 39), who ruled north and south of the Hindu Kush, imitate the winged crown of Khusrau II and even include a countermark of a boar's head, a special emblem of the great Sasanian king.

The emblems in the crowns of both Buddhas and lay personages with a combination of wings, crescents, and globes (Fig. 38) is so close to the symbols of the diadems in these coin portraits of Khusrau II and his Hephthalite subject princes (Fig. 39) that a dating in the late sixth century or early seventh seems a reasonable conclusion. The crowns of the Buddhas and the princely donors are adorned with long ribbons found alike in Sasanian sculptured portraits of royalty and, again, in the diadems of the guests at Balalik Tepe.

Related to this "Sasanian" cycle at Bāmiyān is a large damaged wall painting at Dukhtar-i-Noshirwan some 300 km. north of Bāmiyān, the largest and most complete non-Buddhist painting in Afghanistan (Fig. 40). It represents a local prince, perhaps one of the Hephthalite rulers, enthroned like Khusrau II on his famous cup in the Cabinet des Médailles, seated in the frontal position, resting his hands on a large sword between his knees (Fig. 41). The crown with the head of a beast framed in spread wings resembles the diadem on the coins of the sixth-century Hephthalite prince Shahi Tigin.[7] Certain elements, such as the enframement in blunt debased columns supporting inverted truncated triangles, are familiar forms in the architecture of Gandhāra. This frontal convention for the portrayal of Sasanian kings had already been evolved in the great relief of the Triumph of Shapur I at Bishapur and such early Kushan works as the terra-cotta medallion of Khalchayan (Fig. 16).

At Bāmiyān, carved inside the face of the cliff on either side of the niche of the 35-meter Buddha, are staircases that give access to the summit of the vault and by passageways on three levels to a series of sanctuaries. Directly to the west of the colossus and now almost inaccessible through the crumbling of the rock-cut stairs lies a domed shrine preceded by a spacious vestibule, a complex designated Group D by the French Archaeological Mission. Fragments of large painted Buddha images are still visible on the side walls of the porch, but the most interesting part of the decoration consists of the painting of the ceiling of the shrine's narthex: there, between simulated paintings of roof beams, were depicted row upon row of medallions with pearl borders enclosing motifs such as boars' heads, birds holding pearl necklaces (Fig. 41) — singly or in pairs — and human heads, all literal painted copies from the repertory of designs familiar to us in Sasanian silk weaving, as known in actual fragments in the carvings of the robes of the kings and nobles at Taq-i-Bustan, and, as has been discussed above, in the paintings of Afrasiab (Figs. 29 and 73), Balalik Tepe, and Varaksha (Fig. 42). Among the best preserved of these patterns is a roundel with a boar's head preserved in the Kabul Museum. PLATE P. 89 Originally all of these beast and bird forms were emblems of Mithra and other members of the Mazdean pantheon — the boar's head being one of the many symbols of the Iranian god of victory, Verethragna. The boar's head, it may be added, was also a special symbol of Khusrau II. This is only one factor that would seem to confirm the dating of all the painted decorations within the complex of the 35-meter Buddha in the late sixth or early seventh century.

Although it has been suggested that the fragments of Sasanian silk excavated under completely unscientific conditions at Antinoë may be as

Fig. 39 – Coin of Śri Vasudeva. British Museum, London. Compare p. 94.

early as the fourth century, our first concrete evidence for the appearance of these motifs is in their carved representations in the grotto of Khusrau II at Taq-i-Bustan [8] and in the portrayal of some of these same emblems in the stucco decoration of the royal palace at Damghan.[9] In the boar's head, as in the other painted replicas of woven patterns at Bāmiyān, the form is reduced to a heraldic simplification, emphasized in our example by the completely decorative use of lapis lazuli blue for the animal's head. This abstraction is an illustration of the innate Iranian sensibility for lucid ornamental shapes, a tradition going back to Achaemenid times. We have already seen examples of this same fundamental Sasanian motif with local variations in the similarly painted imitations of textile patterns at Balalik Tepe and Afrasiab. We note that, in the Bāmiyān example, the animal's head is enclosed in a circle of pearls interrupted at the quarters of the roundel by square jewel shapes.

Fig. 41 – Glass bowl with figure of Chosros II. Cabinet des Médailles, Paris. Compare p. 95.

Fig. 42 – Bird holding string of beads in a medallion. Group D, Bamiyan, Afghanistan. Compare p. 95 and below.

An actual woven parallel for the boar's head design at Bāmiyān may be PLATE P. 90 seen in a silk fragment unearthed in the graveyard of Astana in the Turfan oasis. The abstract treatment of the central device is very much the same, but it will be noted that in the Astana silk the roundel is divided at the quadrants, not by the square-cut jewel shapes seen in the Bāmiyān wall painting, but by smaller circles of pearls enclosing crescents. This device linked the medallion to the adjoining circles in the woven fabric, and is present in the rare examples of actual Sasanian weaving, such as the simurg textile in the Victoria and Albert Museum (Fig. 30), as well as in silk fragments found at Antinoë in Egypt but presumably woven in Iran proper. It may be that the type of circular border with the cabochons separating the pearl motif is a variation of the looms in eastern Iran or Central Asia. What is important for us is that actual examples of Iranian silk such as the Astana sample provided the models for painters from Western Turkestan to the borders of China. As noted in the description on Page 89, a debased, probably local, weaving of the boar's head design has also been found at Astana (Fig. 44). In this specimen, the pearls of the medallion, as at Bāmiyān, are separated by squares.

It should be noted, finally, as may be seen in our drawings, that the pattern of birds holding pearl necklaces, found in a number of medallions from the ceiling of Group D at Bāmiyān (Fig. 42), is duplicated in paint-

Fig. 43 – Bird holding string of beads in a medallion frame. Varaksha, U.S.S.R. Compare p. 98.

Fig. 44 – Boar's head medallion. Silk fragment from Astana, Chinese Turkestan. Compare p. 97.

ings of the same motif in the murals of Varaksha (Fig. 43), Pyandzhikent, and Afrasiab. Even such small details as these underline the importance of the role of ancient Soghdian art in the formation of styles of painting at Bāmiyān and throughout Central Asia. The combination of the purely Mazdean emblems of the ceiling decoration with the Buddhist subject matter in the rest of Group D illustrates the same syncretic fusion of iconography and style in this phase of Afghan Buddhist art that we have already witnessed in the ornamentation of the niche of the 35-meter Buddha.

A small group of wall paintings at Bāmiyān appears to provide a nucleus of evidence for the formation of what may be designated as a Central Asian style, a fusion and reshaping of elements of Iranian, Indian, and Gandhāran origin into an independent mode that spread eastward to Kizil and ultimately to Tun-huang. The key to this problem is the Blue PLATE P. 91 Bodhisattva of Group E located a short distance to the west of the 35-meter Buddha. We are not concerned with the iconographical aspects of this painting, whether it is a figuration of the Bodhisattva Maitreya or the Buddha in his transcendent aspect, but solely with the stylistic implications of this beaufitul fragment. An analysis of the various modes combined in this painting will help us to understand how this combination of manners has resulted in the creation of a new and original style of Buddhist art related to and yet separate from the Indian and Sasanian cycles at Bāmiyān. First of all, it is apparent that the hieratic frontality and the massive proportions of the figure are reminiscent of the effigies of enthroned Sasanian kings in Iranian rock-cut sculpture and the Sasanian wall paintings in the niche of the 35-meter Buddha at Bāmiyān, as well as the ruined mural at Dukhtar-i-Noshirwan (Fig. 40). At the same time the fluttering scarves, terminating in swallowtail conventions, seem like an inheritance from the strangely "neo-Attic" drapery of the Gandhāra Bodhisattvas (Ill. 3). An Indian element appears in the abstract shading technique, really no more than a thickening of the contours that can be seen particularly well in the definition of the folds of the neck. It will be noted that the ultramarine background of the composition is filled with patternized lotus buds. This curious convention negating space almost as though to suggest an unreal ambient for a celestial being, was used in one of the great fifth-century frescoes of Ajantā, the "Theophany" of Avalokiteśvara in Cave I (Ill. 23), but here at Bāmiyān space and figure alike have been reduced to what we may describe as a diagrammatic flatness. And indeed the general impression that this wall painting creates is one of heraldic patternization, a suggestion in religious art of the formal abstract splendor of Sasanian textiles. This impression is enhanced by the marvelously decorative formalization of the hair ribbons or kusti into shapes resembling French horns (*cornes de chasse*), immediately suggesting these elements in the cycle at Varaksha (Page 70). What we see here presents a curious parallel to that marriage of Iranian and classical forms that produced the supernally beautiful icons of Byzantium and the Third Rome. Much of the formalization described here is, of course, already present in what we may call the proto-Central Asian style of the chateaux of Balalik and Varaksha (Ill. 15 and Page 70), and this brings us to another element that has been assimilated into the creation of this Central Asian style: the drawing in thin wire-like lines clearly visible in the mask of the deity. It would almost seem that this type of draftsmanship is a perfect illustration for those decriptions of the manner of painters from "the Western Countries," in the histories of Chinese painting of the T'ang period. The members of the Wei-chih clan who, according to the T'ang records, stemmed from either Tokhara or Khotan, were renowned for their drawing in line like "bent and coiled iron wires." This is a mode of delineation that also occurred at Balalik Tepe and Varaksha. One final feature that we should note is the Blue Boddhisattva is canopied beneath a kind of truncated pyramid that is, as already noted, a familiar architectural enframement both in Gandhāra and in the great royal portrait at Dukhtar-i-Noshirwan (Fig. 40).

Fig. 45 – The Bodhisattva Maitreya. Wall painting, Group K, Bamiyan, Afghanistan. See below.

The Bodhisattva of Group E is closely related in style to the decorations of the almost inaccessible decorations of Group K at Bāmiyān (Fig. 45), explored during the last years of Hackin's activity in Afghanistan. The principal wall painting, which we know only in copies, represents a crowned Bodhisattva in the center of what might be described as a mandala, or cosmic diagram. The hieratic formalization and the predominance of the beautiful lapis blue closely approximate the style of the Blue Bodhisattva. The plaited curls, falling to shoulder length, are also present. In the enthroned archangel in Group K we can recognize a further Sasanian element in the use of pearl borders separating the tangent circles of the magic diagram.

In the huge trefoil niche at the western end of the cliff at Bāmiyān stands a colossal Buddha, 53 meters in height. The image, together with the mural decoration of the niche, was probably one of the last artistic undertakings at Bāmiyān. This statue itself, from the point of view of style, is a gigantic enlargement of the typical Indian Buddha figures carved at Mathurā in the Gupta period, ca. A.D. 320–600 (Fig. 46). Like the 35-meter Buddha, the image is modeled in clay on a rough-hewn

Fig. 46 – Figure of the Buddha, from Mathura. Archaeological Museum, Muttra. See below.

stone core, covered with a slip of stucco. As noted in the description of our plate, each one of the stringlike drapery folds that cover the body like a net was separately molded on cords attached to dowels driven into the rock. This formalization of an originally classical garment closely resembles the formula evolved from late Gandhāra statues (Ill. 2) in the Buddha images of Mathurā of the fifth century (Fig. 46). The Bāmiyān statue has a close parallel in the gigantic Nirvāna Buddha at Adzhina Tepe in Tadzhikistan (Fig. 47), assigned by its discoverer, Professor B. A. Litvinskii, to the seventh century. Presumably a dating between the fifth and seventh centuries for the whole complex of the 53-meter Buddha is most acceptable.

The gigantic size of the Bāmiyān statue is an evident allusion to the transcendent nature of the Buddha as lord of the cosmos, a counterpart of the representations of Vairocana that, in enormous scale, are represented in the cave temples of China and the great bronze Roshana of Tōdayi at Nara. The colossus could be described, in fact, as the plastic heart of a mandala, or cosmic diagram, completed by the wall paintings that originally covered the interior of the niche. Indeed, it seems highly plausible to recognize in this complicated iconographical scheme the beginnings of esoteric, or Tantric, Buddhism which we know best from its manifestations in Tibet, Nepal, and mystical sects of medieval Japan. In this very connection, it is well to pause to explain that Tantric Bud-

Fig. 47 – Colossal statue of the Buddha in Nirvana. Adzhina Tepe, U.S.S.R. See above.

dhism, or Vajrayāna, is a ritualistic cult, a faith dependent on magic and mystery and the recitation of auspicious spells, which grew out of Mahāyāna Buddhism in the seventh and eighth centuries as a challenge to the dynamic universal powers of the Hindu gods. At the core of Tantric worship were the Five Dhyāni Buddhas, the cosmic regents of the four directions forming a constellation around Vairocana, their creator and lord of the zenith. They in turn created the Five Dhyāni Bodhisattvas as their emanations to minister to mankind. A borrowing from Hinduism was the assignment of the Tāras, as Saktis, or consorts, to the divinities of the Vajrayāna pantheon, surely a manifestation of the emphasis on sexual symbolism and practice in the Tantric rite. Part of the paraphernalia of Tantric Buddhism are the mandalas, diagrams of the spiritual and material worlds populated by the countless creations of Vairocana, so that the more complicated mandalas would include not only the Five Dhyāni Buddhas but the numberless manifestations of these absolutes in all the worlds. This elaboration of Mahāyāna required a new iconography to illustrate its abstruse concepts, necessitating not only the representation of a host of deities but also a vastly enlarged repertory of the mudrās, or hand gestures, now shaped to set forth the new magic powers and spells of the esoteric ritual. It is certainly possible to see the germ of this complex cosmic Buddhism in the endless defile of painted Buddhas and Bodhisattvas decorating the niche of the 53-meter Buddha at Bāmiyān as well as in the mandalas in the wall paintings of nearby Kakrak.

This scheme of decoration around the 53-meter Buddha comprised representations of a countless host of Buddhas on the side walls and a great number of Bodhisattvas painted on the haunches and soffit of the vault. Under the cusp of the roughly trefoil vault is a series of flying divinities in medallions. As has been noted above, the niches carved for the colossi at Bāmiyān are an adaptation of the iwan of Parthian and Sasanian palace architecture for Buddhist usage. Like the large Iranian entrance halls, they have the effect of welcoming the visitor into the realm of the divine being. It is in the flying Gandharvas, portrayed as though scattering flowers and jewels as offerings to the Buddha, that we discern a special connection with Indian painting of the Gupta period (Ill. 5). The figures in their physical type, their sensuous grace and supple movement, appear like provincial versions of the great wall paintings, notably the two theophanies of Bodhisattvas, in Cave I at Ajantā (Ill. 23). The resemblance extends to the type of jewelry and the striped dhotis worn by the Bāmiyān deities.

The painted Buddha images on the side walls of the niche of the giant Buddha statue in their massive proportions and rounded volume again are obviously based on Gupta prototypes in painting and sculpture. They are in this respect the direct ancestors of portrayals of Buddhas in T'ang China and in the famous cycle of wall paintings which formerly decorated the interior of the Kondō of Hōryūji at Nara.

This same Indian style continues in the cycle of Bodhisattvas painted on the summit of the vault on a level with the head of the great statue and extending over the entire roof of the niche. These figures of the Buddhist archangels have the massive proportions of their Indian prototypes with enormously wide shoulders on a trunk tapering to a leonine waist. The hands of these divinities shaping the mudrās, or mystic gestures, move with the same pliant, flowerlike grace of the great Indian icons. For all their gigantic proportions, these Bodhisattva images, lolling on enormous cushions or baroque thrones, give an impression of world-weary elegance and refinement that anticipates the Manneristic style of Indian Gupta art seen in the last Afghan phase of Buddhist painting and sculpture at Fondukistan.

One final detail of the great collection of wall paintings surrounding the 53-meter colossus is worthy of special notice: this is the figure of a kneeling donor balancing a tray of offerings on his head, an isolated fragment located just below the springing of the vault at the outer edge of the

Fig. 48 – Donor figure. Wall painting in the niche of the 53-meter-high Buddha. Bamiyan, Afghanistan. Compare p. 104.

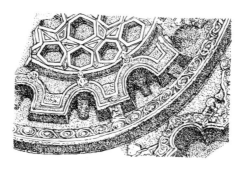

Fig. 49 – Dome of Cave XI at Bamiyan,
Afghanistan. Compare p. 105.

Fig. 50 – Roof of the Temple of Bacchus in ▶
Baalbek. Compare p. 106.

eastern wall of the niche (Fig. 48). The facial type, seen in profile, is
distinctly Iranian. The costume is the same type of mantle belted at the
waist and with wide, peaked lapels that we have already seen in the dress
of the Sun God above the 35-meter Buddha (Fig. 36). We shall once more
encounter this costume, apparently characteristic of the Hephthalite and
Turki peoples who succeeded the Kushans, among the decorations of
Fondukistan, and, with only slight modifications, in the robes of the
princely donors portrayed in the cave temples of Kizil, halfway across
the northern trade route to China (Page 162).

Summing up the evidence for the dating of the sculpture and painting of
Bāmiyān, we have seen that the 35-meter Buddha statue, from its resemblance to early Gandhāra images, might be dated no later than the
third century, but, as also noted above, a later revival of this manner is
perhaps a more plausible attribution. At the same time, the painted decorations of the niche of the smaller colossus and adjoining caves are so
closely related in style, and in the types of crowns worn by the personages,
to Sasanian art of the period of Khusrau II (A.D. 590–628) that a date in
the late sixth or early seventh century appears imperative for the pictorial remains of this complex. As we have also noted, the folds of the
drapery of the 53-meter Buddha are modeled on the robes of the Gupta
Buddha images of Mathurā of the mid-fifth century A.D., and the style
of at least some of the wall paintings in this sector of cliff is derived from
the classical Gupta manner, as seen in the wall paintings of Cave I at

104

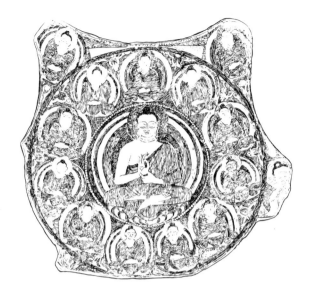

Fig. 51 – Mandala from Kakrak, Afghanistan. Kabul Museum. Compare p. 106.

Ajantā. At the same time, the mannered style and the Tantric character of the Bodhisattva images decorating the niche is so suggestive of the post-Gupta, or Pāla, mode as to suggest a somewhat later dating for the whole complex. Finally, the resemblance of the donor figure discussed above to the Sasanian types of the murals surrounding the 35-meter Buddha that it is possible to suppose that the paintings on the vault of the 53-meter colossus may have been executed at more or less the same time, that is, in the late sixth or early seventh century.

Although, as has been explained in the introduction, Central Asian architecture cannot be treated in detailed fashion, a brief mention of certain architectural features at Bāmiyān is useful to reinforce our conclusions on the different styles of painting and sculpture; for example, in a number of the grottoes adjoining the niche of the 35-meter Buddha are typical Sasanian squinches symbolically supporting the cupola hollowed out at the summit of the sanctuaries. These features are, of course, completely consistent with the Iranian style of the surviving wall paintings of this complex.

Behind the giant feet of the 53-meter Buddha is an ambulatory, from which radiate a number of chapels with simulated structural domes carved into the core of the rock. The decoration of one of these cupolas in Cave XI consists of a kaleidoscopic combination of triangles, hexagons, and diamonds (Fig. 49). The hexagons in this elaborate coffering originally contained stucco reliefs of seated Buddhas, and small heads wearing peaked caps are still visible in the diamond-shaped sections. The effect of the whole, even to the vein pattern at the base of the dome, closely resembles the ceiling decoration of the Temple of Bacchus at Baalbek (Fig. 50). Here, as in the illusionistically painted cubes or parallelepipeds of the niche of the great Buddha (Page 109), is a striking illustration of the longevity of such classical motifs in this latest complex at Bāmiyān.

The precise chronology of the art of the Bāmiyān Valley is a problem difficult to resolve with any degree of accuracy. We have observed that certain iconographic and stylistic elements in the "Sasanian" cycles of painting and sculpture surrounding the 35-meter Buddha point to a date in the sixth and seventh century. Roughly the same period has been suggested for the more Indian style of the 53-meter colossus and the wall paintings of the giant niche. It is obvious, of course, that all of these schemes of decoration were completed before the visit of Hsüan-tsang in 622. It is impossible to suggest that one style, Iranian or Indian, was earlier in date. As appears to be the case in so many sites throughout Central Asia, all may be roughly contemporary productions of different ateliers of workmen trained in a Persian or Indian tradition.

PLATE P. 111 Related to the decorations of the niche of the 53-meter Buddha and to the Bodhisattva of Group E are the wall paintings that ornamented the cave chapels at Kakrak a few kilometers to the southeast of the Bāmiyān Valley. These murals, now removed to the Kabul Museum, could be described as proto-mandalas since, as a forecast of the religious diagrams of Esoteric Buddhism, the predominant theme of these cupola paintings consists of a circle with a central Buddha surrounded by smaller Buddhas in contiguous rainbow-hued body halos or aureoles (Fig. 51). Details of these diagrammatic compositions repeat the Central Asian manner of the Blue Bodhisattva of Group E at Bāmiyān. One section PLATE P. 112 from the décor of a dome at Kakrak, the so-called Hunter King, portrays an enthroned princely personage offering his bow and arrows and hound to the Buddha, presumably in a symbolical gesture of the renunciation of taking life in the chase. Although the painting lacks the refinement of the Blue Bodhisattva, many details such as the formalized hair ribbons and wiry drawing recall the style of the figure of the Bāmiyān cliff. The Hunter King wears a tiara with three crescents. This device resembles the crowns of some of the Hephthalite rulers of Bāmiyān as seen in their coin portraits. Since these coins have been placed in the sixth and seventh century, they may with reservations be accepted as evidence for the dating of the Kakrak wall paintings.

The last significant monument of pre-Islamic art in Afghanistan is the monastery of Fondukistan, dramatically placed on a conical eminence in the Ghorband Valley, a remote and isolated setting that probably saved this religious establishment from the first waves of Arab invaders in the eighth century. The excavation of Fondukistan in the years just before the Second World War uncovered a vihara, with a conventional plan that included a series of chapels for images around an open courtyard. These sanctuaries had been walled up as a precaution against impending danger and to this we owe the extraordinary preservation of both paintings and scores of fragile statues. Each individual cell was a combination of painting and sculpture with the painted background as a continuation and setting for the groups of statues in a sort of Buddhist tableau vivant or illusionistic peep show of the celestial regions. This is a technique anticipated at Bāmiyān and at Hadda and Tepe Marandjan at Kabul, which was destined to spread eastward over all Serindia to China. The theme of each group of statues, including Buddha and Bodhisattva images, was presumably intended as a portrayal of the paradise of one of the divine Buddhas of the Mahāyāna pantheon.

At Fondukistan the medium for sculpture was sun-baked clay, mixed with straw or animal hair as a binding medium and built up around a wooden skeleton or armature. This method approximates the technique anticipated centuries earlier at Khalchayan, where, in a slightly different procedure, an osier shell supported the clay. Actually, the Fondukistan statues were made in the same way as the large mud bricks used for the construction of the fortified manors we see in the Ghorband today. Here, as well as in the architecture of many Transoxian sites, like Varaksha and Adzhina Tepe, big cubes of earth mixed with straw are pressed into shape and built into the ramparts to dry in the sun. The fabric and the effect of the Fondukistan sculpture is totally different from the stucco and stone sculpture of Gandhāra and the Kabul Valley. It is a technique that was employed throughout Central Asia — perhaps even before its sophisticated development at Fondukistan.

The date of the material found at Fondukistan, based on scanty finds of coins of Khusrau II (A.D. 590–628) and a Hephthalite prince of the same period, is certainly no earlier than the seventh century, a chronology borne out by the style of the remarkable painting and sculpture. In both of these media at Fondukistan the same juxtaposition of Iranian, Gandhāran, and Indian forms and designs already noted at Bāmiyān ornamented the facades of the little chapels.

Among these fragments of murals are portrayals of Tāras, the consorts of the Bodhisattva Avalokiteśvara, one light, one dark in complexion, set off against backgrounds filled with conventionalized floral designs.[10] The swelling fullness of the forms and the use of an abstract shading technique as in the paintings in the niche of the 53-meter Buddha at Bāmiyān are completely Indian in character. The same is true of a painting from PLATE P. 113 the facade of Niche E, preserved in the Kabul Museum, with a representation of a Bodhisattva, possibly Maitreya.

Like the Bodhisattvas of Bāmiyān, this figure immediately shows its relationship to the great style of Indian wall painting in its proportions and the S-curve of the torso. A closer inspection reveals at once that this is at the same time a style apart from the classic Gupta manner. The pose has an exaggerated provocative curvature echoed in the affected exquisiteness of the hands and a suggestion of a strange winsome quality in the tilt of the head and the drawing of the pursed, smiling mouth. What we have is a culmination of the kind of Mannerism already suggested in the Bāmiyān Bodhisattvas (Page 110), and only a step removed from the half-erotic, half-mystical conception of religious beings in the art of Tibet and Nepal.

The very first images to be brought to light at this site in 1936 were a series of fragmentary female figures, originally parts of complicated relief compositions, images that at once revealed their Indian character by the soft and sensuous opulence of their anatomical form and the elegant rhythm of their swaying postures. This same predominantly Indian character informs all of the sculptural remains from this monastic foundation.

PLATE P. 114 Particularly beautiful is the seated figure of a Bodhisattva in the Kabul Museum seated in a position of voluptuous ease. The soft modeling of the torso, suggesting the warmth and breathing fullness of the bodily form, is entirely Indian. The lithe curvature of the body and its soft undulation are set off as in Indian sculpture by the precise, even hard definition of the jeweled ornaments. Indian, too, are the exquisite flower-like gestures of the hands and the radiant, sensuous face, like a mask veiled in dreams. The expression at once of radiant serenity and self-contained spiritual calm is the result of essentially the same abstract conception of the godly mask that prevailed in the great icons of Gupta India.

The soft sensuous elegance of the painting and sculpture at Fondukistan has a parallel in the latest cycle of wall painting at Bāmiyān. The giant Bodhisattvas reclining on their massive thrones on the vault of the colossal Buddha are counterparts of this same Mannerist phase of art that

Buddha images. Wall paintings on the east wall of the niche of the 175-ft. Buddha, Bāmiyān, Afghanistan. 5th–7th century A.D.

The illustration shows two of the countless representations of Buddhas that once lined the walls of the niche of the colossal statue. Like the Bodhisattvas painted in the zone above them, the Buddhas and the figure to the right have their hands posed in variations of the *dharmacakra mudrā*. Each Buddha is enclosed in an elliptical aureole. At the left one can make out part of a representation of Maitreya holding his attribute of the begging bowl in the left hand. The globular shapes between the vesicas of the Buddhas are conventionalized lotus blossoms. The white borders surrounding the paintings are recent plaster repairs. Above the row of Buddha images is a curious trompe-l'oeil decoration representing curtains, and, below, a zone of parallelepipeds, such as frequently appear in Roman mosaics and wall paintings (Fig. 80).

109

Bodhisattva. Wall painting in arch of the niche of the 53-meter-high Buddha (east wall), Bamiyan, Afghanistan; 5th–7th century.

Our picture shows one of the numerous Bodhisattva figures that originally decorated the entire arch of the niche above the head of the colossal statue. The divinity, seated with legs folded, is clothed in a *dhoti* and wrapped in scarves; the hands form the gesture of teaching. All these depictions of the Buddhist "archangel," like the Buddha pictures on the side walls, are to be understood as the countless emanations of the cosmic Buddha. Praying figures, painted as half-figures, appear next to the horse-shoe-shaped aureole of the Bodhisattva. The damage done to the paintings by iconoclasts has been repaired with plaster (with spots in our picture). The surviving wall paintings in the large niche are so heavily coated with dust that the viewer can now scarcely obtain an impression of the former brilliance of the colors. However, one is struck by the fact that indigo blue – and Indian color – was used in all the pictures around the 53-meter-high Buddha, while the use of lapis lazuli blue predominated in the picture cycles around the 35-meter-high Buddha. Compare p. 106.

Seated Buddha. Wall painting from the grottoes of Kakrak near Bamiyan, Afghanistan; 7th–8th century B.C. Kabul Museum.

The Buddha is seated in the lotus position; his right hand forms the *vitarka-mudra*. The picture was part of a mandala (religious diagram) of the mystic Buddha that decorated the vault of the rock temple. This figure and the small representations of the Buddha arranged in circle around the central tathagata are to be understood as emanations of it. The columns on either side of the Buddha support panels with representations of small stupas decorated with bands. The Buddha seems to be preaching to the "hunter king," who is pictured directly to the right, next to this picture. (See picture p. 113.) Compare p. 110 ff.

111

The "Hunter King." Wall painting from Kakrak, near Bāmiyān. 7th–8th century A.D. *Kabul Museum.*

The enthroned royal personage placed between adjacent Buddhas is seated cross-legged holding a bow in his folded hands, as though offering this weapon to the Buddhas as a gesture of the renunciation of the hunt. Below and to the left one can make out the figure of a hound and a pair of arrows. The long hair ribbons, ultimately of Sasanian origin, frequently appear at Bāmiyān, as does the crown with three crescents. This latter emblem might make it possible to recognize this effigy as a portrait of a local Hephthalite prince.

Bodhisattva Maitreya. Wall painting from Niche E, Fondukistan, Ghorband Valley, Afghanistan, W. 9½ in. 7th–8th century A.D. *Kabul Museum.*
The figure, light in color, is seated cross-legged (*Lalitāsane*) on a throne; the right hand holds a blue lotus; and in the left is Maitreya's attribute of the lota, or Brahman water flask. The divinity wears a diadem, heavy earrings, not unlike those of the Soghdian rhyton of Plate 6, and hair ribbons of the familiar Iranian type. A necklace and armlets complete his jeweled ornaments.

Seated Bodhisattva. Painted clay. From Niche D, Fondukistan, Ghorband Valley, Afghanistan, H. ca. 72 cm. 7th–8th century A.D. *Kabul Museum.*

The Bodhisattva, like the painted version of the same subject, is seated in a relaxed cross-legged pose. The right hand is posed in the gesture of teaching, while the left hand holds Maitreya's attribute of the water bottle. The material, as in all the sculpture of Fondukistan, is the local reddish clay molded on a wooden armature. The divinity wears an Indian dhoti decorated with circular patterns in powder blue and white. The flesh color, as in all the images from this site, is a tawny red, and the hair is painted a deep blue.

appears like an exaggeration of tendencies inherent in the masterpieces of the Gupta period, approximating the flamboyant aftermath of this golden age with art of the Pāla period (Fig. 52).

When we examine any one of the Bodhisattva figures from Fondukistan, it is as though something of the quality of classical grace occasionally present in Gandhāra sculpture had combined with the more solidly integrated plastic tradition of Indian art to produce a peculiarly moving formula of refined religious expression — in a way, almost hyperrefined — in the manner of late Gothic art. This is a formula that the artist must have found peculiarly effective for expressing the new demand for images that, following the nature of Mahāyāna literature, should be both sensuous and otherworldly. To these ends the Gupta canon of measurement appears exaggerated toward a towering elongation. The gestures assume an even more lyric poetry of movement and the faces, like the masks of Tantric images in Tibet, have a strange expression of inscrutable inner absorption and dreamy sensuality. These images have an air of individuality within a spiritual state, just as in the devotional sects of Buddhism and Hinduism the individual soul retains its identity even in the bliss of union with the Divine.

It should not be overlooked that the elongated canon of proportions of the Fondukistan Bodhisattvas has already been noted in the tall wooden images of Pyandzhikent (Ill. 12). Again, important as an indication of the date and the diffusion of this style, are the fragmentary Bodhisattva images discovered at Adzhina Tepe, a site that we have already noted can be dated with certainty in the eighth century (Ill. 13). These torsos of divinities from Adzhina have the same svelte proportions and the soft treatment that we associate especially with Indian sculpture of the Gupta period. The heads of Buddha from Adzhina (Fig. 32) have a similar resemblance to their counterparts in the Ghorband Valley (Fig. 33). Whether Fondukistan marks the center of this phase of Buddhist art or whether the style was developed in the religious establishments north of the Amu Darya is not of vital importance; what is significant is that we can now be certain that this Mannerist style was flourishing in a region extending from the Hindu Kush region northward into Bactria in the seventh and eighth centuries; and, as has already been suggested, some aspects of this mode were already forecast in the provincial Indian wall paintings of Bāmiyān.

Fig. 52 — Bodhisattva Padmapani. Museum of Fine Arts, Boston. See above.

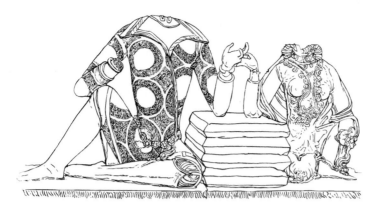

Fig. 53 – Donor figures from Fondukistan, Afghanistan. Kabul Museum. See below.

Still another facet of the international art of Fondukistan is the appearance of elements of eastern Iranian or Soghdian stylistic and iconographic features. Among the sculptures originally placed in Niche E was a pair of donors reclining with one elbow resting on a pile of cushions (Fig. 53), a pose often encountered in the portrayal of royal couples on Sasanian silver plates. The costume of the male figure in this group copies the dress of the donor in the niche of the 53-meter Buddha at Bāmiyān (Fig. 48). His costume is decorated with roundels which, it is reported, originally enclosed stylized human heads as in the painting of Sasanian silk designs at Balalik Tepe. The graceful, tremulously extended hand and the attenuated canon of form, of course, are features also typical of the religious images of Fondukistan.

Fig. 54 – Sun god and moon god. Wall painting, niche K, Fondukistan, Afghanistan. Compare p. 117.

116

Fig. 55 – Griffin. Detail of a wall painting in niche K, Fondukistan, Afghanistan. See below.

This intrusion of Transoxian style and iconography is also found in details of painting from this remarkable site. Among these may be noted a representation of the gods of the sun and moon (Fig. 54), who, long ago, as Mithra and Mao, made their appearance on the coins of the great Kushan dynasty. The mantle of the the Moon God with its wide flaring lapels and the long sword attached to the belt suggests the costume of the solar divinity at Bāmiyān. This is the same type of dress we have just studied on the donor in the niche of the 53-meter Buddha. What is probably the key to the style of this wall painting is the rampant griffin to the left of the planetary gods (Fig. 55): this monster, in the flat, patternized character of the form and the spiraling wing bisected by a pearly band, is very closely related to a similar leogryph found at Varaksha, in a wall painting conceived entirely as an imitation of Sasanian textile design (Fig. 56). This link with the famous Russian site, generally placed in the seventh century, provides a further corroboration of the date of Fondukistan.

Space does not permit more than a brief mention of the Buddha images of Fondukistan. Their style is completely consistent with what we have studied in the Bodhisattva statues. It is not surprising that some of these

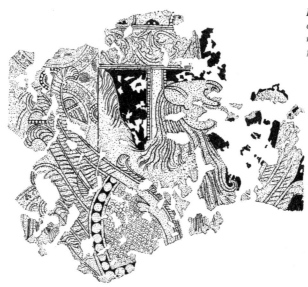

Fig. 56 – Griffin. Detail of a wall painting. Varaksha, U.S.S.R. Compare p. 117.

icons have taken on a strangely attenuated nervous tension that is almost suggestive of the exquisite Gothic Mannerism of such a modern sculptor as Lehmbruck. One of the Buddha images found in Niche D in Fondukistan presents an iconographical problem of great interest (Ill. 24). This is a Buddha dressed in the familiar robe and wearing over it a kind of chasuble set with precious stones. At first this would seem unorthodox, since we have been led to believe that the Buddha renounced all worldly splendor at the time of his Renunciation. It would appear that with the growth of Mahāyāna Buddhism in India, Buddhist icons were decked with splendid robes and even metal crowns to indicate the transformation of the mortal Buddha into a supernatural being. Presently, as in this statue and the images of Pāla India, the bejeweled Buddha comes to represent that transcendent transfigured "Body of Glory," the Sambhogakāya, in which the now divine Śākyamuni reveals himself in radiant splendor to the Bodhisattvas or archangels. Originally this statue at Fondukistan was seated on a lotus upheld by two Nāgas, or serpent deities, so that the original composition must have resembled the Transfiguration of Buddha that we see in a late Gupta sculpture in the porch of the Chaitya-hall at Kārlī.

The facial mask of this image has something of the spheroidal abstraction and radiant benignity of Gupta images. It is particularly close in this respect and in the style of the hair to the seventh-century Buddhist sculpture of Ushkur and Akhnur in Kashmir, which, like the Fondukistan style, combines elements of Indian and Gandhāran origin. Indeed, many of the fragments found at these sites in Kashmir are so nearly identical in style with the Afghan examples that the art of the two monateries appears as part of the same peripheral Buddhist culture that survived beyond the frontiers of India at a time when the religion and its art were dying out in the land of its origin.

1. J. M. Rosenfield, *The Dynastic Arts of the Kushans,* University of California, Berkeley and Los Angeles, 1967, Fig. 121, 131–139, 152–153.
2. Ibid., Pl. IV–IX.
3. Possibly one should read "niches" for "pillars."
4. The technique of the wall paintings at Bāmiyān is the traditional one for Indian cave temples and throughout Central Asia. The rough wall of the grotto was covered with a layer of clay mixed with vegetable fiber to a thickness of from 1.25 to 3.75 cm. This surface was coated with a thin slip of burned gypsum or plaster of Paris. The pigments were applied directly to this ground: they included lapis for ultramarine, red lead, yellow ocher, a green composed of copper silicate, and calcium for white. The colors were applied with animal glue as a binding medium, a substitute for the egg employed in European tempera painting. Cf. R. J. Gettens, "The Materials in the Wall Paintings of Bāmiyān, Afghanistan," *Technical Studies,* VI, 3, Jan., 1938, pp. 186 ff.
5. B. Rowland, *Gandhāra Sculpture from Pakistan Museums,* New York, 1960, p. 10.
6. G. A. Pugachenkova, *Khalchayan, Tashkent,* 1966, Table IV, V.
7. B. Rowland, "The Dating of the Sasanian Paintings at Bamiyan and Dukhtur-i-Noshirwan," *Bulletin of the Iranian Institute,* IV, 1–4; VII, 1, New York, 1946, Figs. 8 and 9.
8. See E. Herzfeld, *Am Tor von Asien,* Berlin, 1920, Fig. 39, Pl. XLIX.
9. Rowland, *Ancient Art from Afghanistan,* New York, 1966, Fig. 9B.
10. *Mémoires de la délégation archéologique française en Afghanistan,* VIII, Paris, 1959, Figs. 200, 201.

VI. SERINDIA

THE KINGDOM OF KHOTAN

Khotan, the name of a modern town on the Khotan Darya to the north of the Kuen-lun range, is a term that is applied not only to this site and the ruins of an ancient royal city to the north of the modern town but also must include various other ancient centers on the southern Silk Road, such as Dandan Uilik, Niya, Endere, and the monastic complex of the Rawak Vihāra, approximately twenty-five miles northeast of Khotan. Presumably all of these ruin sites were at one time within the frontiers of the kingdom of Yotkand, or Odan, the ancient name of Khotan.

Until about A.D. 70, Khotan, together with practically all of the principalities of Serindia, was a vassal of the Hsiung-nu, sometimes identified as the Huns. The skillful maneuvers of the Chinese general Pan Ch'ao in A.D. 73 and 74, in Khotan and Kashgar, displaced the Huns and made possible the installation of a Chinese protector general for Kashgaria, a medieval term used to describe all of western Serindia. The finding of early Kushan coins and Kharoshthi records by Sir Aurel Stein indicates relations between Khotan and the Kushanshahr as early as the first century and helps to support the vague references to the Chinese repulsing an abortive expedition to Central Asia by the Emperor Kanishka. The history of Khotan is punctuated by contacts with China, beginning with the expedition of Pan Ch'ao. In A.D. 202 an elephant was sent to the Han emperor as tribute; in the fifth century a similar gift, sent by the Emperor of Iran, passed through Khotan; again, in 574, a gift of horses was sent to the Chinese court. There are records of ambassadors sent to the T'ang court from 632 to 644. During all these centuries, with only brief lapses, Khotan was apparently a docile member of the Chinese bloc. Wearing a costume resembling the ceremonial robes of the Chinese sovereigns in Yen Li-pên's Scroll of the 13 Emperors,[1] a Khotanese king and his suite are portrayed in a T'ang wall painting at Tun-huang.[2] Following the Tibetan conquest, the history of the region in the ninth and tenth centuries, when the Arabs were overrunning Central Asia, is a complete blank.

A succession of Buddhist pilgrims, beginning with Fa Hsien in the fifth century and ending with Huei Ch'ao in the eighth, have left accounts of their visits. Even in Fa Hsien's day, the desert road to Khotan was arduous and beset with danger. "On the road there are no human dwellings. The sufferings on their journey on account of the difficulties of the way and the rivers exceed human powers of comparison." Two centuries later, Hsüan-tsang relates: "The greater part of the country is nothing but a sandy waste; the arable portion of the land is very contracted. What land there is, is suitable for cultivation, and produces an abundance of fruits. The manufactures are carpets... and fine woven silken fabrics. Moreover, it produces white and green jade... The climate is soft and agreeable, but there are tornados which bring down with them clouds of flying gravel." The pilgrim also refers to the "Indian" character of the written and spoken language and the dominance of the Great Vehicle with a hundred *sangharāmas* and five thousand followers. Hsüan-tsang repeats Fa Hsien's observation of a special reverence for Vairocana and the cult of Vaiśrāvana as a kind of patron saint.

It is evident from the finds of painting, sculpture, and minor arts that Khotanese art was influenced by India, Gandhāra, Iran, and China, and possibly by Chorasmia and Soghdia as well. At the same time, the in-

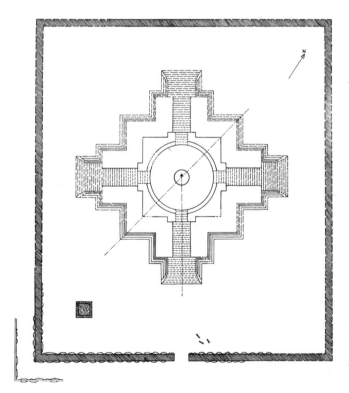

Fig. 57 – Plan of the Rawak Vihara, Khotan, Chinese Turkestan. Compare p. 123

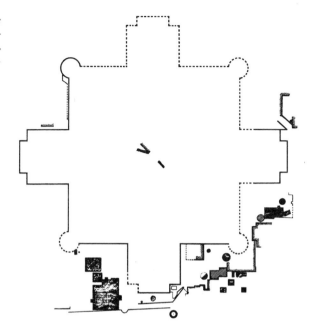

Fig. 58 – Plan of the Kanishka Stupa (Shah-ji-ki-dheri), Peshawar, in Northwest Pakistan. See below.

fluence of Khotan on Buddhist art in China and Tibet is of greatest importance for the diffusion of this conglomerate, cosmopolitan style for the formation of new national artistic idioms. Buddhism was introduced, probably from the Kushan Empire to the west in the early centuries of our era. It is evident that a great many objects from the Khotan area are chance finds, impossible to date or localize accurately, but the scientific exploration of some of the major sites was undertaken by Sir Aurel Stein in the early years of the twentieth century. Later sporadic investigation of the sites by the Otani expeditions led to the discovery of a number of important objects.

To the northeast of Khotan and nearly buried in shifting sands from the fierce desert winds lie the ruins of the monastic city known as the Rawak Vihāra. The stupa itself, which must have risen to a height of over forty feet, was possibly one of the many relic mounds of this type derived from the prototypes in Gandhāra.

The plan of the stupa in the center of the vihara is a large square basement platform with staircases projecting at the quarters so that the ground plan becomes cruciform (Fig. 57). This polygonal layout is close to the foundation shape of the so-called Kanishka stupa (Shahji-ki-dheri) at Peshawar (Fig. 58) and to the ruins of the vast Tope-e-Rustam stupa at Balkh (Fig. 59). This same arrangement prevailed at Parihāsapur

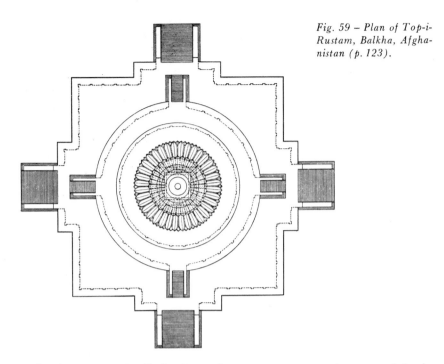

Fig. 59 – Plan of Top-i-Rustam, Balkha, Afghanistan (p. 123).

and other stupas in Kashmir, and we may suppose that an origin in Gandhāra architecture for all of these relic mounds, including the Rawak Vihāra, is highly likely. This close dependence on building plans in the heart of the Kushan Empire is, as we shall see, reflected in the sculptural decoration of the monument in Khotan.

The stupa was surrounded by a vast quadrangle, 164 by 143 feet in dimension. The inner and outer faces of this enclosing wall were richly decorated with colossal stucco images of Buddhas and Bodhisattvas built up on wooden armatures and attached to the wall by massive dowels. In all, Stein uncovered ninety-one statues on the southeastern and southwestern walls of the compound. According to Stein, the destruction of much of this figural decoration was caused not by iconoclasts but by the erosion caused by sandstorms after abandonment of the site; there were indications that at one time the sculptures may have been protected by a wooden roof. Originally, these reliefs were painted as were the spaces of the wall between the figures themselves. It is evident that many of the Buddha images with their voluminous drapery represent the same formalization of a classical garment found in the stucco statues of Hadda and Taxila. However, some of the heads, with their protruding eyes and small, smiling mouths set in a rather dry, conventionalized facial mask,

Fig. 60 – Head of the Buddha from the Rawak Vihara, Khotan, Chinese Turkestan. Metropolitan Museum of Art, New York. See below.

suggest the same abstraction of the classical Gandhāra types found in the sculpture of Tumshuk. It is often impossible to tell with certainty in which direction artistic influences moved over Central Asia, and, in this respect, it is worth pointing out that some of the Buddha images at Rawak display the same blocklike, really cubic simplification of the head and body that distinguishes Gupta sculpture of the fifth and sixth centuries. Supporting the premise of a relationship between the sculpture of the Rawak Vihāra and Gandhāra is a head in the Metropolitan Museum of Art, New York (Fig. 60), reputed to have come from the famous Khotanese monument, which is so close in style and technique to the more conventionalized Buddha heads from Hadda (Fig. 61), even to the

Fig. 61 – Head of the Buddha from Hadda, Afghanistan. Kabul Museum. See above.

method of indicating the curls by lightly punched depressions in the cap-like hair, that this object might be mistaken as a product of the Gandhāra region. Among the coin finds at Rawak were over a hundred issues of the Later Han dynasty, some of which continued in use at least until the fourth century. On the bassis of this evidence and the obvious connections with Gandhāra, it would be possible to place remains at the Rawak Vihāra between the third and seventh centuries, although the close connections with the Gandhāra stucco sculptures make a dating from the third to the fourth century more plausible.

It is certainly possible that some of the statues of Buddha and Buddhist deities at the Rawak Vihāra were intended as replicas of famous miracle-working images worshiped in India. In one fragmentary relief photographed by Sir Aurel Stein we see the central figure enveloped in an aureole containing radiating figures of small standing Buddhas (Ill. 26). The same iconography is presented in a drawing in a banner from Tun-huang, representing a number of sacred images of India, perhaps a copy of the illustrations that, in 641, the Chinese envoy Wang Hsüan-tsê had made for the account of his travels in the Western countries (Ill. 27). Both the Rawak icon and the figure in the Tun-huang painting appear to derive from Gandhāra reliefs representing the Great Miracle of Srāvasti, a prototype for the iconography of Vairocana, filling the cosmos with his mind-made emanations. Vairocana enjoyed a special cult at Khotan, based on the *Avatamsaka Sūtra,* as may be noted in paintings of the cosmic Buddha from this site. A special sanctity was attached to such copies of famous Indian images since they were believed to embody and transmit something of the miraculous qualities inherent in the original. The Chinese pilgrims frequently refer to such replicas of Indian statues brought back to China. It is this cult of miraculous icons in India that accounts for the numerous copies not only in Central Asia but in the Far East of the famous sandalwood image of Udayāna, which according to legend, was made in the Buddha's lifetime. Several statues at the Rawak Vihāra with an eccentric wavelike pattern are presumably attempts to reproduce this venerable idol, which, according to some versions of the story, was drawn from the Buddha's reflection as it was cast on the rippling surface of a pool.

One of the more rewarding sites excavated by Stein in the desert a few miles south of Rawak was the monastery of Dandan Uilik. The finding of Sanskrit manuscripts, including a *Prajñaparamitā* of the Gupta period and a *Vajracchedika* of the seventh or eighth century, in the ruined viharas provides a possible terminus for this site together with the discovery of Chinese coins of the K'ai Yuan (713–42) and Ch'ien Yuan (758–60) eras, although it is highly probable that the artistic remains antedate this literary and numismatic evidence. The innumerable stucco fragments, mainly heads of Bodhisattvas and minor deities, rescued from the sands by Stein's expedition, bear the same relation to their prototypes in Gandhāra as the sculptural remains from Rawak.

Of far greater importance are the paintings of this site. The most interesting of these is known only in photographs and copies made on the spot, since it proved impossible to remove the original from the wall (Ill. 25). The most arresting figure in this composition represents a water sprite or Nāgini in a pose strangely reminiscent of the Venus dei Medici, standing in a lotus tank and accompanied by a small boy. It has been suggested that this detail refers to a legend recounted by Hsüan-tsang of a widowed Nāgini who asked the king of Khotan for a husband in exchange for her protection of the city. The Nāgini and her companion, although defined in a completely linear fashion, have like certain figures at Bāmiyān a strong suggestion of an Indian style in the globelike fullness of the breasts and the sinuous *déhanchement* of the body.

In the upper left-hand portion of this remarkable wall painting appear the figures of a Buddhist teacher, holding a *poshti,* or sacred text, and a monastic companion. Their poses, and notably the stylized elegance of the hands, bear a striking resemblance to the portrayals of seated nobles at Pyandzhikent and, at the same time, anticipate the famous portraits of Shingon patriarchs by the T'ang artist Li Ch'ên and his Japanese followers at Tōji in Kyōto.[3] Visible in the photograph is a stucco image of Vaiśrāvana dressed in scale armor. A recumbent demon lies under the feet of the deity. Insofar as one can tell, this is the same type of laminated mail found in representations of warriors throughout western Central Asia presumably derived from the armor of the Parthian cataphracts. The cult of Vaiśravana at Khotan, predominating in legends reported by both Fa Hsien and Hsüan-tsang, spread to medieval Japan, where his images, like the famous example at Seiryōjii Kyōto, are known as "Tobatsu Bishamonten," the "Tibetan Vaiśrāvana".[4] This divinity, the Kuvera of Indian Buddhist mythology, was one of the Four Guardian Kings, and, as regent of the North, especially appropriate in his adoption as the protector of Khotan.

The finds at Dandan Uilik also included a number of panel paintings probably presented as votive offerings to a shrine. One example in the British Museum, painted on both sides, shows, on one face, a three-headed and four-armed divinity, painted blue and seated on a pair of small addorsed bulls (Page 131). This personage with three heads, two benign, one malevolent, wears a tiger skin loincloth and holds the disks of the sun and moon in the two upper hands, a combination of attributes that, together with the couchant bulls as a throne, would lead us to identify him as Maheśvara. Similar figures appear on the silver salvers of eastern Iranian origin; and the symbols of the sun and moon are also seen in the representations of planetary divinities at Pyandzhikent. The panel of Maheśvara from Dandan Uilik, and also a very similar wall painting of the same four-armed deity from Belavaste in the Khotan oasis,[5] is probably an exemplification of the absorption of Hindu gods into the already Tantric form of Buddhism that flourished in Khotan, possibly as an illustration of the *Lankavatara Sutra* in which the Buddha appears in the guise of various members of the Brahmanic pantheon. Maheśvara as a Tantric emblem of the Buddha's supreme spiritual power was carved at the entrance of a fifth century cave temple (No. 8) at Yün Kang in Shansi Province.[6] The style of the Maheśvara of Dandan Uilik is as closely related to the Indian tradition as the image on the other side of the same panel goes back to Iranian antecedents.

PLATE P. 132   This portrayal of a bearded, four-armed figure dressed in a green mantle and pointed black boots has been identified by Sir Aurel Stein as a divinization of the Iranian culture hero Rustam, not only because of his general Persian appearance and the attribute of the bull-headed mace held in the upper right hand, but also because, at the famous Sasanian citadel of Kuh-i-Khwaja in Seistan, Stein discovered a similar figure paired with a many-armed deity like the one portrayed on the reverse of the present panel. Stylistically the god bears a certain resemblance to cult images of Mazdean type at Pyandzhikent, where, it will be remembered, Rustam enjoyed a cult. It is possible, as some have suggested, that the attributes of a cup and a knife held by the divinity might identify him as a protective spirit associated with the culture of silk in Khotan. In addition to the details already mentioned, the attenuation of the form and the costume present haunting reminiscences of the Soghdian style of Pyandzhikent. The significance of the juxtaposition of this "Persian Bodhisattva," or "Rustam," with the four-armed Mahésvara on the reverse remains a mystery.

PLATE P. 133   Another panel painting from the Ming-oï site of Karashahr should be considered in connection with these panel pictures from Khotan if only because the art of this northern site was closely related to that of Khotan, and the picture in the National Museum at New Delhi reveals the variety of styles displayed by these icons from the two ends of the Silk Road. The

*Fig. 62 — Seated king or divinity.
Hadda, Afghanistan. See below.*

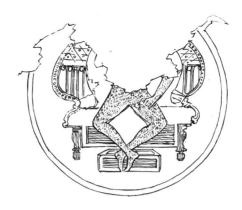

Karashahr panel represents a Bodhisattva seated cross-legged on a massive throne, the back of which rises in a horseshoe arch to form a kind of combination nimbus and enframement for the deity. The pose of this figure and gesture of teaching (*vitarka mudrā*) described by the right hand suggest a possible identification as Maitreya. Representations of the Buddha of the Future in a similar pose are known in Gandhāra sculpture and in countless portrayals of this Bodhisattva in the art of Six Dynasties China. In many ways the style of this panel suggests that fusion of Indian, Iranian, and classical elements seen in the Blue Bodhisattva of Bāmiyān: the hieratic "Sasanian" pose, the scarves attached to the crown, the almost diagrammatically formalized linear drawing, combine with suggestions of the abstract shading of Indian or Late Antique origin. A wall painting discovered at Hadda in the nineteenth century and known only by sketch shows a figure of a king of Bodhisattva seated cross-ankled on a throne with a similar horseshoe back (Fig. 62). The strongly patternized conception of the figure and its setting suggests at once the final Central Asian style of Bāmiyān and the Indo-Iranian quasi-Byzantine manner of Kizil. It is the painted counterpart of the painted sculpture of Shorchuk, which, as we shall see, is still faintly reminiscent of the reliefs of Hadda. The drapery lines of the dhoti are drawn in sharp cursive strokes in a linear shorthand version of the Gandhāra formula. The figure with its violet-mahogany complexion and full form is essentially Indian. In the tiara are the familiar three disks so familiar to us in the headdresses of the figures in the Sasanian cycles at Bāmiyān and Kakrak (Page 112). These details, and the elegance of the hand gesture, make the figure appear as a miniature of the Bodhisattvas of Bāmiyān. The painted panels recovered at Dandan Uilik include several rep-

PLATE P. 134

PLATE P. 135

resentations of a haloed personage riding horses and camels, generally holding a shallow cup in one hand. All must deal with local Khotanese legend.[7] Another one of these equestrian figures can be made out at the lower left of the "Nāgini" mural. A long horizontal panel deals with the story of the introduction of silk to Khotan. The line drawing appears to bear some relation to Chinese technique, but the figures in all are the same combination of Indian and Iranian forms so frequent at Khotan. Other small Buddha figures, painted in a cursive manner, resemble details of fragmentary wall paintings recently discovered at Adzhina Tepe. Among the objects obtained by the Otani expedition of 1910 from the Khotan region, without any definite find-spot, is a gilt bronze Buddha head. This piece is related to the rare examples of metalwork found in Gandhāra proper, except that it is the largest fragment of a bronze statue that has come to light in Central Asia. The resemblance of the idealized, still markedly Graeco-Roman mask to the stone Buddha types of Gandhāra is immediately apparent. One specific detail, the enormously enlarged *ushnisha*, or cranial protuberance, closely resembles the treatment of this magic mark in a number of schist Buddha heads recovered by the Italian expedition at Butkara in the Swat Valley (Fig. 9). This close stylistic and iconographic relationship between the bronze head from Khotan and its counterpart in the early school of Gandhāra carving in Buner and the Swat Valley may offer a clue to the route of Indo-Roman art to Central Asia — as the comparison suggests by way of the passes north of the Swat region by way of Gilgit. In this connection, it perhaps is not without significance that this same type of enlarged, bun-like *ushnisha* appears on the head of Buddha in the preaching scene from Mirān (Page 3). As a footnote it may be added that this same stylistic peculiarity may be seen in the gilt bronze Buddha in the Winthrop Collection of the Fogg Art Museum, generally designated as a Six Dynasties, or T'ang, copy of a Gandhāra statue but very possibly a product of Khotan that found its way to China.[8]

A small group of painted fragments reputed to have been found at the site of Belavaste in the Khotan area present yet another facet of the art of this region. These wall paintings include several subjects of Tantric divin-

---

In this aspect of Siva, the god is represented with three heads, two benign, one malevolent, enclosed in a nimbus. The deity is ithyphallic and wears a tiger skin over his loins. He is seated on two ad-dorsed bulls in a kind of decorative repetition of his vehicle, the bull Nandi. The four arms display the attributes of his power: the disks of the sun and moon are supported in the upper pair of hands; the lower right hand holds a white lotus bud, and the lower left grasps a vajra.

Maheśvara. Painting on wooden panel (obverse). From Dandan Uilik, Khotan, Sanctuary D. VII, Chinese Turkestan. H. 15 in. 6th–7th century A.D. *British Museum, London.*

Rustam or Silk God. Painting on wooden panel (reverse of No. 24). From Dandan Uilik, Khotan, Sanctuary D. VII, Chinese Turkestan. H. 15 in. 6th–7th century A.D. *British Museum, London.*

Bodhisattva Maitreya. Painting on wooden panel. From Ming-oï, Karashahr. H. 15¾ in. 6th–7th century A.D. *Stein Collection, National Museum of India, New Delhi.*
The painting represents a Bodhisattva, probably Maitreya, seated on an ornate throne with a back in the shape of a horseshoe arch. The divinity is seated in European fashion with crossed ankles and is framed in a red halo and mandorla. Scarves, like the *kusti* of the Sasanian in a green painting of Bāmiyān, are draped over the shoulders and arms. The hands are posed in the *dharmacakra mudrā.*

133

Head of Buddha. Gilt bronze. From Khotan, Chinese Turkestan. H. 17 cm. 3rd–4th century A.D. *National Museum, Tokyo.*

Vairocana. Fragment of wall painting. From Belavaste, Khotan, Chinese Turkestan. H. 31½ cm. 5th–6th century A.D. *Museum of Central Asian Antiquities, New Delhi.*

Kneeling Deva or worshiper. Fragment of wall painting. From Belavaste, Khotan, Chinese Turkestan. H. 21 in. 5th–6th century A.D. *Museum of Central Asian Antiquities, New Delhi.*

The heavy bearded divinity, seated cross-legged on a cushion, wears a peaked bonnet, green surcoat, and high black boots. In his upper right hand the god holds what has been identified as a bull-headed mace, an emblem of the Iranian hero Rustam. The lower left hand appears to touch one of the scarves hanging from the cap. The upper and lower left hands grasp respectively a knife and a cup, attributes associated with the Silk God of Khotan in another panel from Dandan Uilik. The gold crown recalls the description of the headdress of the king of Khotan by the sixth-century pilgrim, Sung Yün: "The king of this country wears a golden cap on his head like the comb of a cock; the appendages of the headdress hang down behind two feet and they are made of taffeta about five inch wide." These *kusti,* so familiar to us in the crowns of divinities in Afghanistan and Russian Turkestan, can be seen descending to rest on the knees of the present figure.

This object, one of a number of such fragments of metal sculpture, was collected by the Otani expedition to Sinkiang. A smaller gilt bronze Buddha head of similar type was also acquired by the Japanese at the same site. An unusual iconographic feature is the large ushnisha, which, as explained in the text, is related both to the Buddhist art of the Swat Valley and the wall paintings of Mirān (Fig. 9 and Plate 2). With regard to the gilded surface, it should be remembered that Buddhists considered gold as the supreme color. Probably, as in later Tibetan practice, the bronze was coated with a thin mixture of gold and mercury; when gently heated, the mercury evaporated and the gold clung to the metal image.

The figure is portrayed with hands in the gesture of meditation. The presence of this, and indeed many other portrayals of the Cosmic Buddha, is a clear indication of the predominance of the Mahāyāna doctrine in Khotan. Part of the iconography of the Great Illuminator, who contains all worlds, is the presence of a formalized Mount Meru, a number of vajras, and a winged horse, appearing like so many tattoos on the body. The extremely hieratic treatment of the form is universal in Khotanese religious painting and is prophetic of the style of the mandalas of Tibet and the Far East.

This small fragment presents a kneeling winged male personage, the hands folded in the *añjali mudrā* of adoration. The figure was probably placed at the feet of a now lost Buddha image. The presence of a mysterious eye on the hand has suggested an identification with Indra, who, together with Brahma, is often represented worshiping the Buddha as a symbol of the submission of the Vedic titans to the lord of the new order.

ities, among them an image of Vairocana — his body "tattooed" with various emblems of the universal power. A distinctly Saivite deity not unlike the "Maheśvara" of Dandan Uilik, and aesthetically most pleasing of all, is a little winged genius with his hands folded, closed palms together PLATE P. 136 in the *añjali mudrā.* Of special iconographical interest is an eye that appears on the back of the saint's hand. This attribute, sometimes associated with India, frequently appears in Japanese icons of the Thousand-Armed-and-Thousand-Eyed Avalokiteśvara. Perhaps the most simple explanation of this attribute is that the merciful Bodhisattva has eyes everywhere to see the afflictions of humanity. In style, this figure and indeed the whole group of paintings from Belavaste, is distinctly Indian in character — in type, in the peculiarly soft, boneless drawing of the anatomy, and in the jeweled ornaments. The little angel has a very moving expression of radiant ecstasy communicated not only by the pose of fervent adoration but by the large lotiform eyes and the full smiling lips. The prototypes for this Indian style at Khotan are not to be sought in India proper but rather in the provincial extension of the Gupta manner, which we have already seen at Bāmiyān and Fondukistan (Pages 110 and 112). Another feature, ultimately of Indian origin but exaggerated in the Afghan examples, is the filling of the flat background with conventionalized blossoms.

Stein's excavations in the Khotan oasis uncovered numerous seal impressions with representations of both Indian and classical divinities, indicating positively the presence of Western traders in the early centuries of Khotanese culture. Another chance find, acquired by von Le Coq, is a pottery amphora, which again presents the intrusion of the classical tradition into Central Asia (Fig. 63). Not only is the shape a familiar form in Greek ceramics and metalwork, but the designs embossed in the medallions around the shoulder of the vessel include such classic motifs as palmettes, lion heads, and a silen holding a rhyton. It is quite possible that this glazed amphora is of Parthian origin. Jars of a very similar shape, but with less interesting designs, were found by Pelliot at Tumshuk, covered with a bluish green lead glaze sometimes regarded as an Iranian invention.

The artistic relations between Khotan and China are supported by accounts in the T'ang histories of painting to the effect that famous Khotanese painters came to China in the sixth and seventh century, notably Wei-ch'ih I-sêng, a Buddhist painter who was the marvel of his age for his effects of relief — described as a "concave-convex" mode, a technique that may refer either to his employment of the Indian type of modeling in light and shade or, as is suggested in the famous copy of a lost original in the Museum of Fine Arts, Boston,[9] a technique of building up parts of the composition in gesso, a forecast of a similar technique in later Chinese and Japanese art, as, for example, the *nuriage* of Mōmōyama Japanese screens. This artist is also described as painting in lines like "bent and coiled iron wires," a description that calls to mind the linear manner of the paintings at Bāmiyān and the sites of Russian Turkestan.

Also associated with Wei-ch'ih I-sêng is a scroll in the Berenson Collection, Settignano, again a copy of a lost original probably made before

Fig. 63 – Amphora from Khotan, Chinese Turkestan. State Museums, Prussian Cultural Property, Indian Art Department, Berlin. Compare p. 138.

A.D. 1032.[10] The subject is a series of dancing girls performing a wild measure with yard-long whirling scarves — perhaps a distant echo of Hsüan-tsang's note on Khotan: "The country is renowned for its music; the men love the song and the dance." In this scroll the figures are isolated against the plain background, according to the classic Chinese mode of figure painting, and the types of the dancers are the round-faced T'ang beauties we shall meet again at Astana. But, for all the departures from Wei-ch'ih's original, this late copy serves to illustrate the extraordinary esteem in which the art of Khotan was held in what was for so many centuries the greatest center of painting in the Eastern world.

1. Paul Pelliot, *Les Grottes de Touen-Louang,* Paris, 1914–1921, Pl. CXXXIII.
2. L. Sickman and A. Soper, *The Art and Architecture of China,* Harmondsworth, 1956, Pl. 62.
3. Sickman and Soper, *op. cit.,* Pl. 70(B).
4. Y. Yashiro, *Art Treasures of Japan,* I, Tokyo, 1969, Pl. 150.
5. Bussagli, *op. cit.,* p. 60.
6. O. Sirén, *Chinese Sculpture,* II, London, 1925, Pl. 34.
7. Bussagli, *op. cit.,* p. 59.
8. B. Rowland, "The Iconography of the Flame Halo," *Bulletin of the Fogg Museum of Art,* XI, 1, Jan., 1949, Fig. 1, p. 11.
9. Seckel, *op. cit.,* p. 197.
10. Bussagli, *op. cit.,* pp. 64–65.

VII. SERINDIA

TUMSHUK

Tumshuk, between Marbashi and Aksu, located amidst small mountain chains rising from the plain, to the east of Kashgar, is the only important Buddhist site west of Kucha and also the most mysterious ruin on the northern Silk Road since the name of the city is not mentioned in any early documents. The modern place name, "Tumshuk," is a Turkish word meaning "beak" or "promontory" and was unknown before the fifteenth century. Only a few sections of this extensive ruin field were superficially excavated by Pelliot and von Le Coq. In addition to a series of large reliefs decorating the entrance wall of the cella of a building designated Temple B, explored by Pelliot, a great number of statuettes and heads of Buddhas, Bodhisattvas, and minor deities in clay and wood were recovered by the French and German expeditions. It is assumed that Tumshuk was a Hinayāna complex although a few heads identified as Bodhisattva suggest that the Great Vehicle was also represented.

In the separate panels of the long frieze of reliefs on the base of Temple B, the heads and larger figures were all molded in the reddish local clay and separately attached by wooden dowels to the back of the shallow box-like frame (Ill. 28). It is evident that molds were extensively used both for heads and bodies, and this accounts for the monotony of expression and pose as well as the rather dry imitation of earlier Graeco-Buddhist and Indo-Iranian styles. Although in their attenuation and elaborate ornaments, the figures in the relief of an unidentified scene from the life of Buddha show a resemblance to the art of Fondukistan, they completely lack the sensuous warmth and elegance of the clay images from the famous Afghan site. It is possible that the formula for the expressionless round faces with their small eyes and mouths represents the intrusion of a Chinese influence even in this westerly part of Serindia. The vine and palmette designs that fill the frames of the Tumshuk reliefs are a distant borrowing from similar motifs in Late Antique and Byzantine art. Von Le Coq believed the art of Tumshuk could be placed in the second or third century; Pelliot was in favor of a date in the fourth or fifth. Although there is no internal evidence for dating the Tumshuk sculpture, it certainly could be contemporary with or slightly later than images of

Fondukistan and Adzhina Tepe, in other words, approximately seventh or eighth century A.D., but as we shall see below, there is some evidence for an earlier dating.

There is so little to distinguish between the globular heads of Bodhisattvas from Tumshuk and even details of their elaborate crowns and similar heads from Kizil and Shorchuk that one is almost persuaded to think of an international style extending from Kashgar to the Turfan oasis, over a period of centuries.

The great assortment of sculptural fragments collected by Pelliot at Toqquz-Sarai, the site of the principal Buddhist ruin at Tumshuk, includes heads of Bodhisattvas or devatās. In all of these portrayals of divinities, the lips are pursed in an "archaic smile," a convention that appears universally in the monastic cities of the northern caravan road; the smile, together with the half-closed eyes, had become a cliché for the expression of beatitude and pensive serenity. Some of these attendants of Buddha (Ill. 28 and 29) wear fantastically elaborate crowns with a broad tassle issuing from a large ring, a detail, which, as Mlle. Auboyer has pointed out in her admirable account of the costumes of the Tumshuk figures, may go back to prototypes in Gandhāra and Mathurā (Ill. 31). As we shall discover in our next chapter, not only details such as this but also the bland facial mask relate the clay heads of Tumshuk to types at Kizil and Shorchuk.

In contrast to these somewhat stereotyped divine personifications, other heads from Toqquz-Sarai display an unusual power and individuality.

Such is the fearsome Yaksha, or demon, in the Musée Guimet (Fig. 64). The mask with its wild, deeply set round eyes and the flamelike streaming hair and beard is like an evocation of the antique silens (Fig. 65) that make their appearance in the guise of ascetics or soldiers in Mara's army in the sculptural repertory of Hadda. As the French report on Tumshuk suggests, we may even discern a distant ancestor in the bearded silens on the coins of ancient Panticapaeum. All these belated translations of classical or Gandhāra types into a simplified local expression at Tumshuk would seem to reinforce the connection with Gandhāra rather than with the full-blown baroque phase of the same Graeco-Buddhist tradition at Fondukistan and Adzhina Tepe. Although it is tempting to consider the Tumshuk statuary as a later conventionalized transformation of the elegant baroque tableaux of Fondukistan, it is just as possible that the sculptors of Tumshuk could have arrived independently at their local expression in the universal stucco and clay technique of Gandhāra, even before the Mannerist style of Fondukistan and Adzhina Tepe emerged from the same background.

The resemblances of the Tumshuk figures to the beautiful lithe forms from the famous site in the Ghorband Valley are at best superficial: a similar technique of modeling and molding in clay and a fondness for heavily bejeweled and attenuated forms. At Tumshuk, as we have already noted, the suave sophistication of Fondukistan has turned into a dry mechanical formula. It is, of course, a natural and common failing of art historians dealing with Central Asian problems to struggle to establish

Fig. 65 – Head of a Silenus. From Hamadan, Iran. Formerly Sarre Collection, Berlin. See above.

143

Fig. 66 – Seated Buddha. Sanchi Museum, India. Compare p. 149.

a later date for the material from all archaeological sites east of Gandhāra, forgetting, of course, that the easternmost and earliest of all the Buddhist centers, Mirān, is almost exactly contemporary with the Graeco-Buddhist art of Afghanistan and northwest Pakistan. In other words, in our study of the various Central Asian styles, we are apt to forget the lesson of Romanesque sculpture in France where many different regional

The Buddha is represented seated in yoga posture, his hands folded in the *dhyāni mudrā*. The drapery is more like a sheath, revealing the body beneath. The head and *ushnisha* are represented as simple spheroidal shapes without indication of the individual curls.

The face of the Buddha head is covered with gold leaf; the curls covering the head and ushnisha like a cap are painted ultramarine blue. The hollow in the center of the forehead probably held a crystal or jeweled disk, symbolizing the *urna*.

The divinity wears a wreath of plaited leaves above the ringlets circling the brows. In comparison with the heads from Kizil (Plate 42) and Shorchuk (Plate 45), this Bodhisattva still retains something of the sensitivity of the modeling of the Gandhāra tradition. The treatment of the features and the spiraling curls over the forehead are certainly modeled freehand, in contrast to the dry mechanical formalization in the headdresses of divinities found at other sites on the northern trade route. The closest comparisons for this persistence of the Gandhāra stucco style are to be found in certain heads from Tumshuk, but even there the Late Antique mode has already been translated into a Central Asian idiom.

144

Statuette of seated Buddha. Wood. From the north side of the Great Stupa, Tumshuk, Chinese Turkestan. H. 16.5 cm. 5th century A.D. *Indische Kunst Abteilung, Staatliche Museen, Berlin.*

Head of a Bodhisattva. Painted clay. From Duldul-akhur, Kucha oasis, Chinese Turkestan. H. 31.5 cm. 5th century A.D. *Musée Guimet, Paris.*

Head of Buddha. Painted and gilded wood. From Tumshuk, Chinese Turkestan. H. 12.5 cm. 4th–5th century A.D. *Indische Kunst Abteilung Staatliche Museen, Berlin.*

147

styles developed within a period of about one hundred and fifty years, and it is not always possible to assume that the later church carvings were influenced by earlier or contemporary monuments: all in their different ways evolved from a common dependence on the techniques of Roman sculpture, the devices of manuscript illumination, and inheritances from the Carolingian period. To repeat, in a similar fashion, it is entirely plausible to think of the art of Tumshuk and other sites such as Shorchuk coming into being through contacts with Gandhāra long before this same tradition, combined with Indian ideals, produced the

Buddhist reliquary. Wood covered with painted cloth. From Kucha, Chinese Turkestan. H. 31 cm. 4th century or later. *National Museum, Tokyo.*
This extraordinary object, acquired by the Otani expedition, is possibly from Subashi, where other caskets of a similar shape have been excavated. The reliquary consists of a circular box with a conical lid. The drum of the casket is painted with a frieze of dancers wearing animal masks, perhaps performing a shamanistic ritual. The lid of the box is decorated with medallions enclosing winged and tonsured erotes playing musical instruments. These circular frames are filled with pearls as in Sasanian textile design, and the style of the music-making amorini is reminiscent of the angels of the Mīrān frescoes (Fig. 6). Between the roundels are heraldic birds, again suggestive of prototypes. The reliquary on a small scale seems to present us with an epitome of all the various stylistic elements that produced the hybrid styles of the Kucha oasis. The object resembles the conical relic-containers represented in a wall painting entitled "The Division of the Buddha's Relics," formerly in the Māyā Cave at Kizil (Fig. 25). The technique appears to be litharge, an oxide substance added to the paint to produce a hard varnish finish, like lacquer in appearance. It is related to the *mitsudaso* medium of the famous Tamamushi Shrine of Hōryūji at Nara.

painted and sculptured chefs d'oeuvre of Fondukistan and Adzhina. The conclusion to be drawn from this digression is that the decorations at Tumshuk could very possibly be dated as early as the fifth century, the chronology originally proposed by Pelliot. As we shall see, some of the chance finds from the site, perhaps imports from the West, very clearly bear out such a dating.

Among the treasures of the Central Asian collection in Berlin is a wooden statuette of a seated Buddha. Although dated as early as the second or third century A.D. by von Le Coq, the figure is without any question either an import from India or a close copy of an image of the Gupta period. Its closest prototype is a statue of Buddha at Sāñchī (Fig. 66), dated A.D. 450. As in the image at Sāñchī, the drapery of the Tumshuk figurine falls from the wrists to form upright V-shaped conventions over the folded legs. The little wooden statue has something of the blocky quality of Kushan sculpture, but the soft, delicate modeling of the body, as seen through a transparent *sanghatī*, recalls the uninterrupted smooth surface planes of some of the great masterpieces of Gupta art at Sārnāth, and the face of the Enlightened. One with a wonderful expression of absorption in seraphic vision is very delicately carved like a miniature version of the Sārnāth formula of the fifth century.[1]

PLATE P. 145

Another rare example of wooden sculpture from Tumshuk is a gilded Buddha head in a quite different style. It reminds us immediately of the conventionalized type of Buddha to be seen in countless examples of stucco sculpture from Adzhina Tepe (Fig. 32), Hadda, and Fondukistan (Fig. 33). The face retains something of the feeling of aliveness and spirituality of the best Gandhāra art in the subtlety of the carving of the features to a far greater degree than the faces of the clay icons from

PLATE P. 146

Tumshuk. The possibility that this object, like the gilt bronze Buddha head from Khotan discussed in an earlier chapter, may be an import from Gandhāra cannot of course be excluded.[2]

The presence of these two exotic wood carvings at Tumshuk, both presumably to be dated in the fifth century, provides an argument supporting the same approximate chronology for the whole site, but, as has been suggested above, the unmistakable resemblance of the clay sculpture to the style of Fondukistan should persuade us to bracket the work at Tumshuk between the fifth and seventh centuries.

PLATE P. 147

Duldul-akhur, briefly explored by Pelliot, is geographically in the Kucha oasis, but the fragments of sculpture from this Buddhist sanctuary, such as the head of a Bodhisattva, are more closely linked to the style of Tumshuk. In comparison with the heads from Kizil (Page 171) and Shorchuk (Page 183), this Bodhisattva still retains much of the sensitivity of modeling of the Gandhāra tradition in stucco and clay sculpture. The features as treated and the spiraling curls over the forehead are certainly modeled freehand, in contrast to the dry mechanical formalization notable in the masks and headdresses of divinities found at other sites on the northern trade route. The closet comparison for this persistence of the Gandhāra stucco style is to be found in heads from Tumshuk, but, as we have seen, even there the Late Antique mode has already been translated into a Central Asian style.

1. Rowland, *Art and Architecture*, Pl. 83.
2. The discovery of a carved wooden head, presumably in Group G at Bāmiyān, confirms the existence of wooden images in Afghan Turkestan. (This object is in the dépôt of the Musée Guimet.)

VIII. SERINDIA

THE CHIVALRIC ART
OF KUCHA AND KIZIL

The ancient kingdom of Kucha dominated the northern caravan route and, in the seventh century, became the capital of the Chinese government of the Tarim basin. From the artistic and political point of view it included the sites of Kumtura, Tumshuk, and Duldul-akhur. The pilgrim Hsüan-tsang has left us an account of the luxuriant fertility of this oasis: rice and corn were plentiful; the arbors, heavy with grapes; the orchards produced pomegranates, plums, pears, peaches, and almonds in abundance. In the days of its glory the culture of Kucha was international in character with elements of Iranian, Indian, and Chinese civilizations and religions. Like most of the Buddhist centers on the northern trade route, Kucha was stubbornly devoted to Hinayāna Buddhism, and not even the eloquence of Hsüan-tsang could shake the Sarvastivadin monastic scholars from their aversion to the doctrine of the Great Vehicle. This kingdom was renowned for its music and the beauty of its women; as Hsüan-tsang relates: "They excel other countries in their skill in playing on the lute and pipe. They clothe themselves with ornamented garments of silk and embroidery." But not all was pageantry and courtly splendor: in the cave paintings at Kizil in the Kucha oasis we are reminded more than once of the emphasis on the transitory vanity of human life, always uppermost in the rigid ascetic doctrine of the Sarvastivadins: as in the Medieval Dance of Death, a skeleton embraces a court lady (Fig. 67); death's heads appear entwined in floral motifs; and, in one memorable fragment (Fig. 69), a monk contemplates a skull with all the rapt ecstasy of a Franciscan friar by Zurbarān.

As will be seen, something of the splendor of this chivalric society, continually on the alert against the encroachment of the Turkish Khans, is reflected in the wall paintings of its rock-cut monasteries. The influences that shaped the various styles that flourished in the oasis came from India and Gandhāra, Afghanistan, and the transformed Iranian art of the Transoxian regions, so that, in many ways, this culture may be regarded as an eastward extension of the earlier Kushan styles and techniques.

Fig. 67 – Death and courtesan. From the "Cave with the red dome," Kizil, Chinese Turkestan. Compare p. 151.

PLATE P. 148 One of the most remarkable objects from the Kucha region is a relic casket now in the collection of the National Museum in Tokyo. This reliquary was obtained by the Otani expedition, presumably at Subashi, northeast of Kucha and Kizil. The casket is a cylindrical box surmounted by a cone-shaped lid. It may be noted that reliquaries of the same shape are represented in a wall painting at Kizil, illustrating the division of the relics of the Buddha (Fig. 25). No painted decoration, not even the famous wall paintings at Kizil, presents us with such a synthetic combination of all the various elements of the style of Central Asian art. The ornament of the lid is particularly revealing in this respect. Nude winged erotes are enclosed in roundels of an unmistakable Sasanian form. The cupids with their shaven heads and evocations of the Late Antique manner of Gandhāra immediately remind us of the winged genii of Mirān (Fig. 6). The border of the enclosing medallion with pearls separated by cabochons is another imitation of eastern Iranian silk designs, such as we have already noted at Bāmiyān (Page 89) and Russian Central Asia. The outer rim of the lid of the reliquary contains the repeated motif of an oval surrounded by small dots, another borrowing from the repertory of Sasanian textile design. The drum of the Kucha reliquary is painted with a frieze of elaborately costumed dancers wearing demon,

152

Fig. 68 – Monk with death's head. From the "Cave with the red dome," Kizil, Chinese Turkestan. State Museums, Prussian Cultural Property, Indian Art Department, Berlin. Compare p. 152.

bird, and hare masks. Some of these bear a marked resemblance to beast masks, worn by the dancers at the dedication of the Great Buddha of Tōdaiji at Nara in 752, now preserved in the Shōsō-in Collection. As Hsüan-tsang and other visitors noted, Kucha was renowned for its music and dancing, and what we see here is presumably a rather accurate recording of the performance of a funerary ritual dance tending toward exorcism, a subject that would have a certain appropriateness for the function of the casket as a container of saintly relics. The style of this painting has a daring movement, and the foreshortening of the figures to suggest the wild rhythm of the ballet is almost realistic in comparison to the formalized Indo-Iranian mode of the Kizil wall paintings. However, we shall encounter once again the general flatness of the forms and the conception of the figures, like suspended mannequins with their feet hanging straight down in the famous Knights from the Cave of the Sixteen Sword-Bearers (Page 162). The combination of Late Antique and Sasanian with Indo-Iranian elements suggests that this fascinating object may well be one of the earliest examples of the Kucha style, certainly no later than the sixth century of our era.

The chief glory of ancient Kucha is preserved for us in the great collection of wall paintings recovered from the grottoes of Kizil by arduous labor

153

and a miracle of improvised techniques for removal and packing by von Le Coq and his associates. Although lamentably great portions of this priceless material were lost with the destruction of the old Museum für Völkerkunde during the bombing of Berlin, a sparse but choice collection of smaller mural panels survived and as displayed in the galleries of the museum at Dahlem they now form the finest collection of Central Asian wall painting and sculpture in the Western world. These murals present us with an astonishing pageant of Kuchean society — kings and queens, knights and ladies, monks and artists, all included in seemingly endless cycles of wall paintings dedicated to the Buddha, his saints, and his legend.

Our knowledge of the civilization of Kucha is based largely on the paintings and sculptures decorating the Buddhist rock-cut temples at Kizil, located to the west of the modern town in the wild ravines of the Muzart Tal River. The Ming-oï — "Thousand Houses" — of Kizil, like their counterparts at Bāmiyān, are hewn out of the soft sandstone of the mountainside. Although the plans of the individual caves differ from the layout of the typical Bāmiyān grottoes, the complexes at Kizil were connected by interior galleries and staircases. Today the openings of the ancient chapels resemble so many dark natural caverns in the eroded, deeply striated face of the cliffs rising abruptly from the floor of the valley. In one of the dramatic photographs taken by the German expedition we look out of a monastic cell at very much the same landscape that spread before the eyes of the Buddhist community fifteen hundred years ago.[2] Directly below are rocky escarpments furrowed into deep gorges by the river that winds into the middle distance, a green and fertile plain with orchards of peach and apricot. In the distance rises an awesome mountain background, barren and deeply scarred with crevices by centuries of erosion. No wonder that von Le Coq, like Hsüan-tsang before him, spoke of the beauty and bounty of the Kuchean oasis: "Happy memories of fruitful work in glowing weeks of summer weather" — interrupted, as at every site on the edge of the Taklamakan Desert, by demonic sandstorms that plunged the noonday sun into Stygian darkness.

The people of ancient Kucha are described as Tocharian, sometimes identified with the Yüh-chih of Chinese tradition. They used an Indo-Germanic language, related both to European and Indo-Iranian tongues. However, the relations of the Kizil styles with western Central Asia and the problem of dating the wall paintings of Kizil are at best conjectural matters. Although the styles represented at this site, both the semi-Indian manner and the highly decorative rainbow-hued Indo-Iranian or pure

"Central Asian" mode, appear to have been anticipated in the wall paintings of Bāmiyān, which I am inclined to date from the fifth to the seventh centuries. Local imitations of these Kizil styles appear in some of the earliest caves at Tun-huang, assigned by most scholars to the late fifth and sixth centuries. If we are to rely on the chronological evidence of the murals in the Caves of the Thousand Buddhas, it would, of course, be necessary to relegate all of the stylistically related Buddhist wall paintings to the west of this famous Chinese site to an earlier period. There is, of course, the possibility that all were done at the same time and the further possibility that the heraldic elements in the Six Dynasties paintings at Tun-huang traveled westward to affect the style of Kucha itself. There is one other possible and perhaps more convincing solution to this dilemma. If the Bāmiyān wall paintings were completed in the sixth or early seventh century and the reflections of the art of this famous center of Buddhist art at Kizil date from approximately the same period of A.D. 500 to 600, then the chronological relationship with the dateable material at Tun-huang of the sixth century becomes more plausible. It also becomes evident immediately, by the same token, that it is not necessary to presuppose any great time-lag for the transmission of artistic styles across the Silk Road in these last centuries before the Islamic invasions. As may be seen in the portraits of donors in the wall paintings at Kizil, the Tocharians were European rather than Mongol in appearance, with light complexions, blue eyes, and blond or reddish hair, and the costumes of the knights and their ladies have haunting suggestions of the chivalric age in the West.

What better introduction to the cycles of painting at Kizil could we have than by one of the artists themselves? In the grotto, appropriately called the "Painter's Cave," we see the master himself (Fig. 69), a dapper little figure scarcely less stylishly dressed than his courtly patrons. He has shoulder-length hair and wears a close-fitting short tunic, a tight belt supporting a short sword, knickers, and neatly laced sandals. He wields a long, pliant brush and holds a paint pot in his left hand. Other similar "self-portraits" by the painters of the Kizil murals have their names annotated in cartouches, an assertion of individuality in Central Asian art that we have already encountered in Tita's signature at Mirān.

The various styles of painting in the Kizil grottoes appear to have their

Fig. 69 – Painter. From the "Painter's Cave," Kizil, Chinese Turkestan. See above.

antecedents in the cycles of murals at Bāmiyān, which once again looms as the center for the diffusion of Indian, Iranian, and classical forms along the trade routes over Serindia.

The so-called Indian style at Kizil is related to the vast assembly of Buddhas, Bodhisattvas, and minor deities painted in the niche of the 53-meter Buddha at Bāmiyān. At Kizil we have a Serindian version of the same provincial Indian style. The Indian types and costumes illustrated on Page 157 are a Central Asian adaptation of the great wall decorations of Ajantā. Here, as at Bāmiyān, the shading of the forms takes on even more the appearance of a decorative reinforcement of the contour lines, and the figures themselves are drawn with less feeling for the suave anatomical articulation of the Gupta forms.

PLATE P. 158 Fragments like the portrayal of a youthful ascetic from the Cave of the Navigator have a superficially Indian look in the social type and Brahmin chignon but the mask has taken on a distinctly Central Asian character in the oval face, the greatly elongated eyes, and — in a universal trait — the depressed nose, looking almost as though broken at the bridge. The portrayal of the muscular structure is certainly related to the schematic appearance of the completely Indo-Iranian manner predominating in the Kizil grottoes.

PLATE P. 157 The detail from the Peacock Cave is perhaps the most convincingly Indian in the whole Kizil cycle. This group of sword-bearing figures are recognizable Indian ethnic types. The ambitious use of both profile and three-quarter views and the overlapping of the forms in three distinct planes has echoes of the Ajantā compositions as well as the arrangement of Gandhāra relief sculpture. The drawing in fine, sinuous lines takes us back to the Flying Divinities of Bāmiyān (Ill. 5). The color scheme, limited to ocher, white, and copper green, is different from the palette employed at Bāmiyān, and the flat areas of tone without shading are again comparable to many of the details in the niche of the 53-meter Buddha.[3] All of the Indian-style paintings at Kizil already show a fondness for the flat patternization of the figures and an emphasis on linear definition, which has much in common with the more typical Serindian techniques developed at this famous site.

The style for which Kizil is chiefly famous is generally designated Indo-Iranian to describe the elements that comprise it. Actually, as can easily be seen by comparison of our illustrations, there are many varieties within this style in which the essential ingredients manifest themselves in different proportions. This style, or these styles, are to be recognized as an original Kuchean assimilation and translation of many foreign forms and

Figures holding Swords. Fragment of wall painting from the Peacock Cave, Kizil, Chinese Turkestan. H. 22 in. 6th–7th century A.D. *Indische Kunst Abteilung, Staatliche Museen, Berlin (Dahlem)*. The figures are arranged in three overlapping rows, a device often employed to suggest spatial depth in Gandhāra reliefs. They hold short swords painted malachite green and assume histrionic rather than martial attitudes. It is possible that the subject represents Siddhartha learning the art of war or, perhaps more likely, the dispute of the Mallas for possession of the relics of the Buddha.

Young ascetic. Fragment of wall painting from the Cave of the Navigator, Kizil, Chinese Turkestan. W. 13¾ in. 6th–7th century A.D. *Indische Kunst Abteilung, Staatliche Museen, Berlin (Dahlem).*
This fragment is an example of the Indian manner that flourished in the Kucha oasis, side by side with the various Indo-Iranian styles. Not only the type and the Brahman topknot, but also the use of abstract reinforcing the outlines, is of Indian derivation. White highlights on the nose and eyelids heighten the illusion of relief.

Devatā and Gandharva (celestial musician). Detail. Fragment of wall painting from the Cave of the Frescoed Floor, Kizil, Chinese Turkestan. W. 53 in. 6th–7th century A.D. *Indische Kunst Abteilung, Staatliche Museen, Berlin (Dahlem).*
The divinity at the left wears an elaborate crown with three jeweled disks, from which hang serpentine ribbons. What appears to be an *urna*, a magic mark usually reserved for the Buddha, is painted on the forehead. Long intertwined scarves, a torque, and strings of jewels ornament the nude torso above the dhoti. The gandharva at the right with a dark complexion, perhaps intended to suggest an Indian rather than an Iranian type, strums a bow-shaped harp. The face is given a suggestion of relief by the strident white highlights. In the detail of the skirt at the lower right the folds are indicated by parallel stringlike loops, as in many examples of late Gandhāra sculpture. A thicket of floral patterns fills the background above the celestial couple. An unusual technical feature of this fragment is the deep incision of the lines of the preliminary drawing into the surface of the wall.

Frieze with Ducks in Medallions. Detail. Wall painting from the Largest Cave, Kizil, Chinese Turkestan. H. ca. 45 cm. 6th–7th century A.D. *Indische Kunst Abteilung, Staatliche Museen, Berlin (Dahlem)*.

A clay bench some 50-cm. high ran around the side wall of the cella of this cave, reminiscent of the banquettes in the palaces of Varaksha and Afrasiab. The medallions enclosing beribboned ducks holding pearl necklaces in their beaks formed the decoration of this base for the support of now vanished Buddha images. Another fragment from the same frieze is in the collection of the Hermitage, Leningrad. This decoration of heraldic birds in roundels, together with other similar fragments found by Oldenburg at Toyuk, is a clear indication of the extraordinarily accurate copying of Sasanian textile patterns in Eastern Turkestan and shows us unmistakably one of the ingredients that went into the formation of the Indo-Iranian style in Eastern Turkestan.

Preaching Buddha. Detail. Wall painting from Upper Cave, Ravine 2, Kizil, Chinese Turkestan. 6th–7th century A.D. *Indische Kunst Abteilung, Staatliche Museen, Berlin (Dahlem)*.

The Buddha in the center of the composition is represented seated, his right hand raised in the *vitarka mudrā*. Above him are the figures of Indra and Brahma. At the proper left appears a three-headed six-armed representation of Maheśvara. A number of devas and lokapalas fill the upper left-hand corner of the composition. At the lower left appears a demonic figure holding a small child. A

160

monk kneels in supplication at the feet of the Buddha. The story apparently illustrates the miracle when the Buddha persuaded the cannibalistic yaksha to spare the life of the child of the king of Atavi, who, in order to save himself, had offered daily sacrifices to the monster until only the young prince remained as ransom. The present wall painting is only one of many such scenes of preaching and miraculous intervention that once lined the walls of the grotto.

Knightly Donor. Fragment of wall painting from the Cave of the Sixteen Sword-Bearers, Kizil, Chinese Turkestan. H. 63 in. 6th–7th century A.D. *Indische Kunst Abteilung, Staatliche Museen, Berlin (Dahlem).* This is only one of a long defile of noblemen that once covered the entrance corridor of the cave. The chevalier wears a long mantle with wide flaring lapels. The coat is faced with silk of flowered design and wide borders of varied patterns. Below the upper garment one can see the knight's tapered trousers and painted boots. He carries a long, straight sword attached to a belt of disks, probably leather, reminiscent of those seen in Kushan royal portraits. The costume is related to the dress of the donors of Bāmiyān and Fondukistan (Figs. 48 and 53). The nobleman holds a short dagger in his left hand; the right hand may have held a floral offering. A kind of purse or pocket is attached to the belt below the right arm.

techniques into a true Central Asian manner. As has already been suggested, whether this so-called Indo-Iranian mode is later than or contemporary with the provincial Indian style at Bāmiyān and other Afghan sites, is a question that cannot be answered categorically. For example, from the Cave of the Painted Floor, the famous fragment representing a Devatā and a Gandharva, a celestial musician (Pl. P. 159, Fig. 70), presents many analogies with the so-called "Blue Bodhisattva" of Bāmiyān (Page 91). Here is the same eclectic combination of elements of Iranian, Indian, and classical origin, the same presentation of the forms as flat shapes against a spaceless background, like a textile of floral forms. We find lingering traces, too, of the now completely conventionalized abstract shading of the Indian tradition and the sensitive wirelike drawing that seems to be an adaptation of a style of draftsmanship already present in the wall painting of a ritual feast at Balalik Tepe (Ill. 15). It may be noted, too, that in the dusky musician of this panel the convention of strident white highlights, more decorative than functional, had already been anticipated in the small fragments of mural decorations in the grottoes of Fouladi, a few kilometers to the south of the great cliff at Bāmiyān.

In the fragment under examination, the blue scarf of the musician with its stringlike folds is a reminiscence of a late Gandhāran abstraction of a classical garment; the tiara with fluttering ribbon has its antecedents in the Sasanian styles at Bāmiyān (Page 88) and Varaksha (Page 70).

What is most striking about this style, in addition to its patternization and reliance on exquisite and brilliant mineral colors, is the presentation in terms of a wirelike draftsmanship that only serves to enhance the abstract conception of form. The round faces with small delicate features here as in many other frescoes from Kizil appear to represent distinctive Central Asian or "Tocharian" types.

One may imagine that the brilliance of the colors and the almost diagrammatic simplification of forms and settings at Kizil may have been conditioned by the very darkness of the chapels these murals adorned. In a setting only partially lighted through the front entrance of the grotto, or by torches, this arrangement may well have been calculated to make the Buddhist epics clearer to priests and pilgrims. Again, the dazzling gaudiness of the polychromy of paintings and sculptures alike was designed to attract the visitor by its posterlike clarity. At the same time it is necessary to assume that the decorative disembodied nature of the representations of both earthly and celestial forms is part of a style developed to express appropriately the otherworldly nature of divine beings.

PLATE P. 160

Evidence of direct Sasanian or eastern Iranian influence is not lacking at Kizil. A long horizontal frieze from the front of a clay bench in the Largest Cave is a painted reproduction of a typical Sasanian textile motif such as we have already seen at Bāmiyān and the sites of Russian Central Asia. In the Kizil fragment we have a succession of typical Sasanian medallions with pearl borders; each roundel encloses a formalized portrayal of a duck, beribboned and holding a string of pearls in its beak. The roundels are linked by smaller circles of pearls enframing a crescent, as in actual surviving examples of Iranian silks and their representation at Varaksha (Fig. 43) and Afrasiab (Fig. 73). We could wish for no more direct proof than this that decorators of the grottoes of Kucha were completely familiar with pure Sasanian or Soghdian forms; and it is undoubtedly from this source that much of the patternized quality in the Kizil paintings derives.

A detail from the Upper Cave in the Ravine presents a composition that, with slight variations, is repeated a number of times on the walls of this grotto: Buddha, preaching, and surrounded by diverse personages divine and human. The style of this wall painting represents one of the many variants of the so-called Indo-Iranian manner at Kizil. The composition with superimposed rows of figures symmetrically flanking the central Buddha is an arrangement often seen in Gandhāra reliefs. The forms are drawn with the same wiry lines already noted in other fragments, and the general impression would be that of flat patternization, were it not for the use of a schematized chiaroscuro that consists in reinforcing the contours of faces, torsoes, and limbs with an intense orange pigment. This method serves to give the individual figures a suggestion of volume but, beyond the connotation of space indicated by the overlapping of the rows of divinities, the forms appear to exist on the surface plane. Characteristic of this Central Asian style, which we have already seen, are the round faces and the stiff mannequin-like articulation of the bodies. Another constant feature, here as in other examples of the Indo-Iranian mode, is the exotic brilliance of the tonality.

The iconographical conception of the painting with Hindu divinities as attendants is probably no more than a symbolical allusion to the submission of the Brahmanic titans to Śākyamuni, and not, as in pictorial presentations of the *Lankavatara Sūtra,* of the Buddha's assuming the forms of the members of the Hindu pantheon.

The same insistence on form as a disintegration of substance, and the reduction of all pictorial elements to pattern, is illustrated even more strikingly by the wall painting of a knight from the Cave of the Sixteen Sword-Bearers. Here is a style of almost heraldic simplification: the figures have the flatness and insubstantiality of the royal family of playing cards. This wall painting represents a group of royal donors. The style of the picture, like that of Byzantine art, is a mixture of elements of classical and Near Eastern origin. It will be noted that space as a pictorial factor does not exist. Figures, foreground and background, are all parts of a formalized pattern in a single plane. This characteristic is even more emphasized by the way in which the "sky," and ground around and behind the figures, is filled with a repeated lotus-bud motif, as unreal as the design of a carpet. The figures, like their Byzantine counterparts, appear to be standing on tiptoe, and their existence is noted only in terms of the eccentric silhouettes of their flaring mantles and pointed boots. We are more conscious of the textile designs than the structure of drapery folds and forms beneath. The only surviving classical element in the representation of these figures is the suggestion of arbitrary shading in the reinforced orange contours of the faces. The frozen rigidity of these

PLATE P. 162

Fig. 71 – Jataka scenes. From the "Cave in Gorge R," Kizil, Chinese Turkestan. Compare p. 167.

forms and the reduction of every element to a textilelike design are an inheritance from the Near East, specifically from the Iranian art of the Sasanian period, or the offshoots of that style, in ancient Soghdia. One should add to this the fact that there was no aesthetic feeling for the beauty of the human form as a physical organism in Turkestan, any more than there was in the art of the medieval West.

An abstract, decorative form, strangely prophetic of Matisse, appears in the paintings from the Cave of the Frieze of Musicians. The detail reproduced from the *Rupavati Avadana* is certainly only a more refined variation of the style of the Devatā and Gandharva on Page 171. The forms and their setting have been reduced to an arrangement in line and flat tone: the brilliance of the copper greens and lapis blues is dazzling, contrasting with the chalky white of the flesh tones and the dark flower-

166

strewn ground. Together with the floral forms in the background, which appear like so many conventionalized asterisks, the figures are only decorative details in a magnificent flat pattern, isolated like the shapes in a Greek red-figure vase painting against the black ground. As can be seen by reference to the drawing of Figure 71, the forms are placed in the interstices of serrated leaf shapes, which themselves framed other episodes from the Avadana or Jātaka tales.

This was a special type of religious landscape painting developed at Kizil, a mode that has no antecedents nor any marked influence beyond Kucha. It is an arrangement for the narration of Jātaka stories, as on the ceiling of the Cave in Ravine R; each episode is enclosed in a merlon-shaped frame, so that the complete composition is divided into innumerable separate space cells (Fig. 71). The effect of these regularly repeated serrated leaf shapes is more that of a complicated foliate or flowered tapestry than a mural decoration in the usual sense of the term. It is possible to regard the individual chevron shapes as formalized mountains. In this respect, they have a certain resemblance to the sawtooth mountain conventions seen in the earliest wall paintings at Tun-huang (Page 207), conventions that the T'ang historians of painting scornfully referred to as mountains like "the teeth of a rhinoceros horn comb." It is barely possible, as some scholars have suggested, that the merlon-shapes at Kizil are derived from the creneleations of ancient Iranian tradition, such as crowned the battlements of Khalchayan and the sanctuary of Surkh Kotal.

The dome of the Cave of the Ring-Bearing Doves, completely recon- PLATE P. 172 structed in the Berlin Museum, is only one of a number of such painted cupolas painstakingly removed by the German expeditions from the grotto temples of Kizil and Shorchuk. The prototype for this iconography of Buddhist deities filling the dome of a sanctuary is to be found in one of the shrines of Group C at Bāmiyān, in which pairs of walking Buddhas, framed in ultramarine aureoles and separated by columns, decorate the rock-cut cupola.[4] Although the decoration of the walls of this chapel from Kizil, with subjects such as the Seven Jewels of the Cakravartin — a symbolical reference to Śākyamuni as World Ruler, the First Sermon at Sārnāth, and other scenes of Buddha preaching — is a completely Hīnayāna scheme, the arrangement of the dome with four Buddhas, alternating with four Bodhisattvas, certainly contains implications of a Mahāyāna concept, such as the deployment of the Buddhas of the Four Directions and their Bodhisattvas in fully developed mandalas of the Great Vehicle. Since in the analysis of religious paintings of the traditional periods in the East as in the medieval West, it is never proper or possible to offer the explanation of the artist's combining figures of divinities solely for reasons of balance or decorative caprice, we can only conclude that, at Kizil and elsewhere, such domical compositions contain a symbolical reference to the ancient oriental concept of the Dome of Heaven, filled with images of the transcendent Buddhas and Bodhisattvas. From the point of view of style, the types of Buddha and Bodhisattva heads, color scheme, and the drawing of the figures in combination of thin line and faint suggestions of abstract shading, correspond to what we have seen in other examples of the so-called Indo-Iranian manner in the Cave in the Ravine (Page 161) and the Cave with the Frescoed Floor (Page 159).

The sculpture of the Kucha oasis, which would include finds from Kizil, Duldul-akhur, and Kumtura, is presumably exactly contemporary with the wall paintings and provides a close plastic counterpart for the styles of these murals. There is also an undoubted relationship with the stucco sculpture of Tumshuk and Shorchuk in the ultimate dependence on Gandhāra styles.

PLATE P. 173   A splendid and typical example of sculpture from Kizil is the head of a Bodhisattva from the Cave of the Statues, perfect in the preservation of its polychromy. The type with the small penciled moustache and the princely crown is derived from the royal Bodhisattva images of Gandhāra. In every respect, the head represents the same formalization of earlier classical forms seen in the Kizil wall paintings. The locks of hair arranged in repeated figure-eight convolutions framing the brows and cheeks are a misunderstanding of Late Antique curls. There can be little doubt that the bland, completely symmetrical mask was fashioned with a mold. With only slight variations the identical formula is repeated in other heads from the same site. There is a certain decorative originality in the fantastic crown, in which a tassle-like ornament emerges from a lotus ring and a completely stylized wreath covers the top of the head. This is a type of diadem that also adorns the heads of deities from Kumtura and, as suggested by the comparison with a head from Mathurā, is of ultimate Indian origin (cf. Ill. 29, 30, 31).

The paintings discovered at Kumtura southeast of Kizil appear to reveal traces of Chinese T'ang influence to a far greater degree than the Kizil murals, but the painted clay sculpture from this site could be described as belonging so the same "International Style" as the Kizil wall paintings. In the figure illustrated on Page 174, the long robe, worn over a skirt or dhoti, has certain analogies to the painted sculpture at Kizil. The cross-legged pose, of course, is highly suggestive of the Maitreya iconography of both Gandhāra and Chinese Buddhist sculpture. Indian elements remain in the dark complexion and the soft pliant pose of the body. The tonality with dominant reds and greens is closer to the Chinese decorations in the Turfan region than the cool mineral palette of the Kizil wall paintings. The flowered pattern of the robe calls to mind Chinese textiles of the T'ang period and the painted representation of such designs at Tun-huang.

As has already been noted, the beautiful head of a Bodhisattva from Duldul-akhur (Page 147), although from a site in the Kucha oasis, is more closely related to the style of the transplanted late Gandhāra sculpture of Tumshuk.

The civilization of Kucha, and with it the religious community at Kizil, came to an end with the disastrous Chinese punitive invasion of 648. On that day, the lutes and pipes of Kucha were stilled forever. The flower of Tocharian chivalry fell in the desert dust. With this subjugation of the Tocharian kingdoms of Central Asia, which included the fall of Turfan and Khotan, the old Indian and Iranian styles disappeared forever, and thus, in the last monastic centers at Kumtura and Turfan an almost purely Chinese style prevailed.

1. Subsequent Chinese exploration at the caves of K'o-tzu-erh-ming-wu, west of Kucha, has added little to our knowledge of the problem of the styles already known at Kizil. (Mentioned by Huang Wen-pi in a report for the Chinese Academy, Peking, 1958.)

2. See E. Waldschmidt, *Gandhāra, Kutscha, Turfan*, Leipzig, 1925, Taf. 26.

3. At Kizil, the technique of the mural decoration closely followed the method found at Bāmiyān. The dominant colors were lapis lazuli blue, copper silicate green, iron oxide red; the white gypsum ground usually served for the white areas in the composition. A sooty charcoal gray was used for darker passages in the painting. This palette differs from the pigments used at Tun-huang, where azurite was substituted for lapis and ground malachite for green. (Cf. R. J. Gettens, "The Materials in the Wall Paintings from Kizil in Chinese Turkestan," *Technical Studies, VI, 4, April,* 1938, pp. 281 ff.

4. B. Rowland and A. K. Coomaraswamy, *The Wall-paintings of India, Central Asia, and Ceylon*, Boston, 1938, Pl. 2.

The exact subject of this small painting is not positively identifiable, but obviously portrays a scene in a previous incarnation when the Bodhisattva slew himself to save the life of a child by the kneeling woman at the left. The composition is framed in a conventionalized chevron mountain shape. It is one of sixty-five such separate Jātaka panels arranged in eight rows on the haunch of the vault of the cella. As our drawing, Fig. 71, shows, these multiple serrated panels were linked together to give a collective decorative effect, not unlike a complex foliate wallpaper pattern.

In the eight gores of this melon dome are represented alternate figures of Buddhas and Bodhisattvas. Nāgas support the lotuses on which the Buddhas stand; some hold sacred jewels (cintamani) in their hands. Demonic figures attend the figures of the Bodhisattvas. A lotus blossom is supended over the head of each figure. The Bodhisattvas wear tiaras with three disks, a distant echo of the headdresses of the divinities at Bāmiyān and Kakrak. At least one Bodhisattva, wearing the Brahmanic topknot of an ascetic and holding a flask, might be identified as Maitreya.

This head of a Bodhisattva is remarkable for the nearly perfect preservation of its polychromy. The type, with the small penciled moustache and princely crown, is ultimately related to the royal Bodhisattvas of Gandhāra. In every other respect the head represents the same formalization of earlier classical forms seen in the Kizil wall paintings. The locks of hair, arranged in a repeated figure-eight convolution framing the brows and cheeks, are a misunderstanding of Late Antique curls. There can be little doubt that the bland, completely symmetrical mask was fashioned with molds. With only slight variations the identical formula is repeated in other heads from the same site. There is a certain decorative originality in the fantastic crown, in which a tassel-like ornament emerges from a lotus ring within a completely formalized wreath covering the top of the head.

This unusual sculpture represents a seated personage with legs crossed at the ankles, wearing a magnificent gold-bordered robe of flowered silk. The figure has long black locks falling below the shoulders. The right arm, broken above the elbow, probably reached down to hold some votive offering in the lap. The figure was attached to the corner of a gallery or balcony and presumably represents a lay personage. The long robe, worn over a skirt or dhoti, has certain analogies to painted sculpture at Kizil. The pose, of course, is highly suggestive of the cross-legged Maitreya inconography in Chinese Buddhist sculpture. Indian elements remain in the dark complexion and the soft pliant pose of the body. The tonality with dominant reds and greens is closer to the Chinese work in the Turfan region than the cool mineral palette of the Kizil wall paintings.

Avadāna of Rupavati, or a scene from the Sutasoma Jātaka: the Sacrifice of the Bodhisattva. Fragment of wall painting from the Cave of the Musicians, Kizil, Chinese Turkestan. H. 12 in. 6th–7th century A.D. *Indische Kunst Abteilung, Staatliche Museen, Berlin (Dahlem)*.

Dome from the Cave of the Ring-bearing Doves, Kizil, Chinese Turkestan. 6th–7th century. A.D. *Indische Kunst Abteilung, Staatliche Museen, Berlin (Dahlem).*

Head of Bodhisattva. Painted clay from the Cave of the Statues, Kizil, Chinese Turkestan. H. 38 cm. 6th century A.D. *Indische Kunst Abteilung, Staatliche Museen, Berlin (Dahlem).*

Corner figure from balcony. Painted clay. From main hall, Kumtura, Chinese Turkestan. H. 61 cm. 8th century A.D. *Indische Kunst Abteilung, Staatliche Museen, Berlin (Dahlem).*

IX. SERINDIA

SHORCHUK AND TURFAN

The end of the Central Asian Tradition

The desolate temples and Ming-oï ("The Thousand Houses") of Shor-chuk located on the northern caravan route between Kucha and Ka-rashahr were for a span of centuries a strategic junction for the meeting of influences from East and West. The quantities of sculpture recovered from the sand-buried shrines and abandoned grottoes by Stein and von Le Coq represent a variety of styles and span perhaps as much as half a millennium in date. It is evident that formative influences came from Kucha and, perhaps by way of Khotan, borrowings from the style and technique of Gandhāra. Other examples of sculpture in the universal Central Asian medium of painted clay display a countercurrent of in-fluence from China and Turfan.

On the basement wall of a sanctuary at Shorchuk, Stein uncovered a series of reliefs in the combination of clay covered by a shell of stucco, the traditional method of the chloroplasts of Hadda (Ill. 32). The group illustrated is composed of figures enveloped in clinging robes with the drapery conventionalized into a network of stringlike folds, a formula reminiscent of late Gandhāra images and even more closely resembling the statues of the Rawak vihāra. The photographs taken during the cursory excavations undertaken at this site by Baron Oldenburg display the remains of complicated reliefs filled with densely crowded figures in several planes, an arrangement that in the depth and pictorial character of these plastic tableaux suggests the clay relief panels of Tumshuk.

In one of the shrines (G 4) explored by Baron Oldenburg at Shorchuk (Simsim), the walls of a narrow chapel corridor were completely covered with clay reliefs of a great host of divinities, rising tier upon tier from floor to roof. This astonishing Baroque composition, unlike anything else in Central Asia, with the possible exception of the frieze at Khalchayan, is known to us only in old photographs.[1] In its complexity and sug-gestion of movement, this assembly of divine beings in high relief has an astonishing resemblance to some of the overpowering sculptural en-sembles of Hindu shrines such as Khajuraho and Konarak.

The torso of a Bodhisattva or deva from Shorchuk on Page 183 is an illustration of this same Central Asian Gandhāra style. The attenuation and torsion of the body appear like a rather clumsy eastern imitation of the Hadda-Taxila manner. The deeply incised folds of the skirt reveal a vaguely classical pattern, although it is obvious that the formula is no longer fully understood, so that the organization of the folds is neither consistent nor convincing. It is evident that this group of sculpture from Shorchuk must represent an early phase of the Buddhist art of the Shorchuk-Karashahr area, since, as will become apparent immediately, the many pieces collected by von Le Coq in the cave temples are in the orbit and period of the culture of Turfan and T'ang China.

As in so many of the sites we have visited eastward from Afghanistan, the interiors of the cave temples at Shorchuk were composed as religious tableaux combining painting and sculpture around the principal object

PLATE P. 174 of worship. A single example, a Devatā from the Nakshatra Cave, demonstrates this method of decoration. Superficially with her heavy crown and massive earrings, the long locks of azure hair carries us back to the exquisite sculpture of Fondukistan (Page 114) an impression heightened by the coloristic brilliance of the adoring Devatā. But there the resemblance ends. The completely symmetrical face, a duplicate of others in the same series of figures from this grotto, was undoubtedly made with a mold and has at least a generic resemblance to masks of the divinities of Kizil (Page 173) and Duldul-akhur (Page 147). In the present example, however, the often sensitive modeling of the more westerly sites has given way to a smooth surface treatment; this quality, the definitely spheroidal character of the head, and the cylindrical arms suggest a Central Asian approximation of the plastic style of the T'ang period in China.

Belonging to the same general style and period, but somewhat more ingratiating in the greater softness of execution, is the beautifully preserved seated Buddha from the Kirin Cave. The graceful flowing lines of the incised drapery folds follow a formula familiar to us at Fondukistan (Ill. 24). The hair covering the skull and *ushnisha* is rendered in patternized swirling flame shapes, a completely decorative reworking of the flowing locks of the Gandhāra Buddhas, occasionally seen in certain stucco heads from Hadda and Taxila. As in the case of the Devatā discussed above it is impossible to arrive at anything more than an approximate dating of about 600 to 800 for this sculpture. The Shorchuk Buddha provides one more example of the extraordinary longevity of the Gandhāra style in literally every Buddhist community east of the Pamirs. Certainly the floral decoration of the Buddha's throne would not be out of place at Tun-huang and, again, as in our examination of the bust of the Devatā, the swelling roundness of the plastic treatment combined with the elegant and realistic modeling of the left hand inevitably suggests the Chinese T'ang sculptor's adaptation of the canon of Gupta art in India.

The extremely decorative wall painting of an assembly of Buddhist PLATE P. 186 monks from the Ming-oï site of Shorchuk belongs within the Chinese sphere of influence in the Turfan region of the eighth century and later. The disciples in their canary yellow robes are portrayed in two registers, their hands folded in prayer. The fact that those in the front are shorter in stature may simply indicate that they are younger novices, so that the whole composition is not to be interpreted as an example of reverse perspective. The figures are all conceived in terms of line and flat tone with thin, wiry brush lines, drawn with a certain delicacy and assurance, but with the same formula of surface conventions of strokes for the drapery structure repeated in each figure. The heavy-jowled round faces, all of them types, have a distinctly Mongol cast. The only trace of Western influence in this provincial example of T'ang painting is to be seen in the roundel decoration of the yellow robes, a Chinese transformation of Sasanian textile design.

When, in the early seventh century, Hsüan-tsang journeyed to Kao-ch'ang he traversed a vast desert tract, where "there are no birds overhead, and no beasts below; there is neither water nor herb to be found . . . through which the only means of observing the way (was) the heaps of bones and the horse dung." Tormented by mirages of great armies maneuvering in the sands and by demons riding the howling winds, he finally made his way to the capital where the king endeavored to persuade the pilgrim to become his palace chaplain. Probably, even in this time, the oasis was only able to survive through an elaborate system of *karez,* or subterranean irrigation tunnels, as Stein suggests in his description of the universal desolation surrounding modern Turfan and its ruin fields. The Turfan oasis, or basin, lies to the north of the Taklamakan Desert in the shadow of the Kurak-tagh range, in a sort of vast natural amphitheatre through which passed the "New Caravan Road" opened for trade with the West as early as the Han period. Kao-ch'ang (later known as Khocho or Kara-khoja or Qoco) was the capital of the region as early as the first centuries of our era. From its geographical position beyond the western hinge of the Great Wall, Turfan was always subject to Chinese influence, both political and artistic, and at the same time subject to inroads by the Turkish hordes and later the Tibetans. In no other

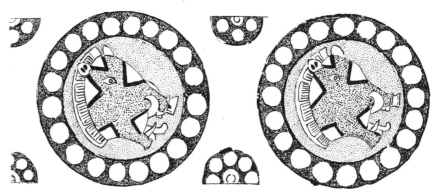

Fig. 72 – Boar's head medallion. Toyuk, Chinese Turkestan. Compare p. 179.

Central Asian site is it more possible to trace artistic developments as parallels to political change than in Turfan. In the beginning both the people and language of Turfan were related to the Indo-Iranian culture of Western Turkestan, but with the ascendancy of the Ch'iu dynasty of Chinese origin in the fifth century there began a gradual process of "Sinification," culminating in the conquest of Turfan by T'ai Tsung's armies in 640. From then on, until the Uighur occupation of 843, Turfan and its art were to all intents and purposes a province of T'ang China. During the Uighur domination Manichaean and Nestorian establishments vied with Buddhism, until the end of the ninth century, when Buddhism, characterized by Tantric influences from Tibet, enjoyed a revival, that lasted until the Moslem and Mongol invasions.

The term *Turfan* embraces a great number of separate sites, both re-

Fig. 73 – Boar's head medallion. Detail of a wall painting, Afrasiab (Samarkand), U.S.S.R. Compare p. 179.

178

ligious and secular, representing every phase of the development of art in Eastern Turkestan. We know the art of the region through the efforts of the German expeditions of von Le Coq and Grünwedel and the extensive excavations by Sir Aurel Stein in the early decades of our century.

The principal sites excavated by von Le Coq and Stein include the cave temples in the red sandstone cliffs of the gorge of Toyuk, and ruins of the Uighur capital of Kara-khoja, twenty miles east of Turfan, the Buddhist grottoes in the picturesque valley of Bazählik, the defile of the Kizil-Tagh, east of Kara-khoja. Both Stein and the Japanese expedition under Count Otani explored the graveyard of Astana at the outskirts of ancient Kao-ch'ang.

Each of the successive centuries of culture in the Turfan oasis reveals a completely different and separate stylistic character. The earliest remains of sculpture and painting from such sites as Murtuk and Toyuk are distinctly "Western," a combination of Indian and Iranian elements, with only slight suggestions of Chinese influence. At Toyuk, for example, the German expedition discovered a frieze of painted boars' heads in medallions (Fig. 72), a completely formalized version of a motif originating in Sasanian textile design and also found in the painted decorations of Bāmiyān (Page 91) and Afrasiab (Fig. 73).

The wall paintings from the shrines at Murtuk, east of Turfan, clearly demonstrate the Chinese domination of the art of this region as early as the eighth century. The rather strident rainbow hues of the detail of a Buddha image illustrated on Page 187 display a tonality totally different from the cool, mineral palette of the Kizil murals. Both the types and the

Fig. 74 – Horse. Chinese grave figure. Fogg Art Museum, Cambridge, Mass. Compare p. 180.

取尤冶容求好君子所仇結恩而絶寝

此之由

Fig. 75 — Ku K'ai-chih, detail from the scroll, "The admonition of the instructress to the court ladies." British Museum, London. Compare p. 189.

Fig. 76 — Yen Li-pen, scroll of portraits of thirteen emperors, detail. Museum of Fine Arts, Boston. Compare p. 190. ▶

color scheme are comparable to the cycles of painting of the T'ang period in the Thousand Buddha Caves at Tun-huang. The actual choice of the dazzling combination of colors is only another different attempt to suggest the radiant splendor of the celestial realms by the sheer brilliance of the tonality, a device independently arrived at by the mosaicists of Byzantium and the Italian religious artists of the late Middle Ages.

PLATE P. 188 Indicative of the variety of styles, all of them ultimately of Chinese origin, is another fragment of Buddhist wall painting from Khocho, the Kao-ch'ang of Hsüan-tsang's epic journey. Enough remains to enable us to identify the episode of the Great Departure, which had been popular in China as early as the fifth century, in the reliefs of the grottoes of Yün Kang. The heavy proportions of the Bodhisattva are completely typical of the T'ang figure style, and Siddhartha's steed with its long mane and lean neck repeat an ideal of animal proportion seen in countless grave figurines of the T'ang period (Fig. 74). Again completely Chinese is the sure and sweeping line drawing.

Although there are minor variations in plan and elevation, many of the temples at Bazählik repeat the typical form of the grottoes at Kizil, with a square cella enclosing a stupa, preceded by a porch or open gallery. At

Turfan some of the chapels were hollowed out of the rock, but others were freestanding wooden structures built against the side of the gorge, sometimes with all or part of the cella cut into the wall of the cliff.

Whereas the art of Kucha and other westerly sites on the northern trade route were exclusively dedicated to Hīnayāna Buddhism, in the Turfan region wall painting and sculpture alike were devoted to Mahāyāna themes. Many show Tantric elements introduced from Tibet in the ninth century. One of the favorite subjects at Bazählik was the representation

Torso of a Bodhisattva or Deva. Painted clay. From Shorchuk, Chinese Turkestan. 5th–6th century A.D. or earlier. *Indische Kunst Abteilung, Staatliche Museen, Berlin (Dahlem)*.
The figure, nude from the waist up, wears a skirt or dhoti still vaguely reminiscent of a classical garment. It was probably a part of a large relief composition, such as those uncovered by Oldenburg, Stein, and von Le Coq, in their explorations of the Ming-oï of Shorchuk. It is possible that the rather heavy blue and green of the skirt represents a later overpainting.

This and other similar half figures of divinities were originally installed in niches some two meters above the floor, as if to suggest that they were adoring the Buddha from the skies. The devatā wears a heavy diadem above the coiffure arranged in incised gore shapes and massive earrings. Billowing behind the figure is a voluminous mantle framing the deity like an aureole. The hands folded in *añjali mudrā* hold two blossoms as offerings to the Buddha.

The pedestal is decorated with two wreaths of conventionalized flowers enclosing winged deer, perhaps a local variation of the Sasanian roundel pattern. The Buddha is represented seated in the yoga posture, the left hand holding a fold of his mantle. The missing right hand probably described the *vitarka mudrā* of teaching.

in gigantic scale of the Manushi Buddhas, repeated endlessly in the temples explored by von Le Coq and Stein (Ill. 33). The Manushi Buddhas are the predecessors of Śākyamuni, who appeared in the world in a succession separated by vast aeons of time. The number of these paracletes varies from five to as many as fifty-two in Mahāyāna texts. In Tibetan and Nepalese Buddhism they are believed to be imbued with the essence of the cosmic creator, Adi Buddha, and at their death or Nirvāna were reabsorbed into the godhead. One, Dipankara Buddha, enjoyed particular popularity because during his earthly mission he prophesied that his devotee Sumati would one day be reborn as the historical Buddha Śākyamuni. A number of these large wall paintings, recovered by von Le Coq, were imbedded in the walls of the Museum für Völkerkunde in Berlin, where they were completely destroyed during the Second PLATE P. 193 World War. Others of the same type recovered by Aurel Stein from adjoining caves, but more severely damaged, are exhibited in the Museum for Central Asian Antiquities in New Delhi. The arrangement in all is invariable, with a large Buddha treading on lotus blossoms flanked by donors and divine personages.

From the stylistic point of view it is evident at once that these murals belong to the period when the art of the Turfan region was completely dominated by the influence of T'ang China. Although the basic composition of a central Buddha, surrounded by attendants in smaller scale, goes

Bust of a Devatā. Panited clay. From the Nakshatra Cave, Shorchuk, Chinese Turkestan. H. 53 cm.
7th–8th century A.D. or earlier. *Indische Kunst Abteilung, Staatliche Museen, Berlin (Dahlem).*

Seated Buddha. Painted Clay. From the Kirin Cave, Shorchuk, Chinese Turkestan. H. 66 cm. (figure); H. 32.5 cm (base). 7th–8th century A.D. or earlier. *Indische Kunst Abteilung, Staatliche Museen, Berlin (Dahlem)*.

Group of Monks. Wall painting from Ming-oï site (M. XIII), north of Shorchuk, Karashahr, Chinese Turkestan. W. 29½ in. 8th–9th century A.D. *Museum of Central Asian Antiquities, New Dehli.* This fragment was removed from a small sanctuary, which may have been a Buddhist theological seminary. The group of disciples in the present wall painting is probably to be considered in connection with other panels representing aged Buddhist teachers from the same cave.

This is a detail from a row of nearly identical seated Buddhas, dating from a period when the area was completely under Chinese influence. Both the heavy plastic type and the rainbow brilliance of the colors have many parallels in the T'ang art of Tun-huang.

186

Seated Buddha. Detail. Fragment of wall-painting from Temple 19, Murtuk, Turfan, Chinese Turkestan. 7th–8th century A.D. *Indische Kunst Abteilung, Staatliche Museen, Berlin (Dahlem)*.

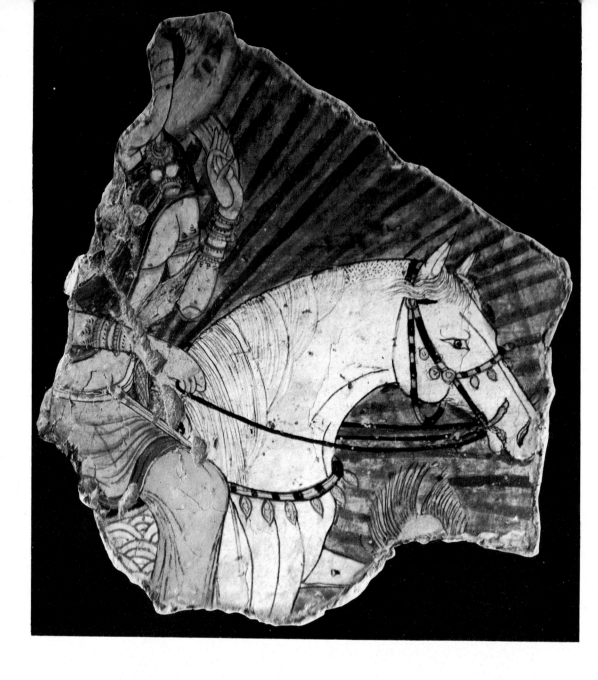

The Great Departure. Fragment of wall painting. From Khocho, Turfan, Chinese Turkestan. H. 10¾ in. 9th century A.D. *Indische Kunst Abteilung, Staatliche Museen, Berlin (Dahlem)*.
This fragment originally decorated the central rosette at the summit of a temple cupola. The picture relates the legend of Siddhartha, mounted on his horse Kanthaka, fleeing from his father's palace at Kapilavastu to renounce the pomps of the world. The Bodhisattva's left hand is raised in the mudrā of teaching. The figure is circled by a sunburst nimbus.

back to precedents in the art of Gandhāra, and a few scattered details such as winged helmets and types of armor, are vaguely reminiscent of Sasanian motifs, the style as a whole is unmistakably Chinese. Not only do the bland spheroidal masks of the Buddha and attendants reflect the T'ang transformation of the Gupta style but the essentially linear character is not notably different from what we see in paintings of the seventh and eighth centuries at Tun-huang. These huge panels have a distinctly flamboyant, Baroque quality in their crowded, intricate compositions and the somewhat lurid palette of reds, blues, greens, and maroons. Such minutiae as the conventionalized floral forms and drapery patterns are again derivative of T'ang formulas.

The Tantric ogress, or Dākinī, illustrated on Page 194 is another masterpiece of the T'ang style in this last phase of Central Asian art. The assurance of the draftsmanship expressing at once fullness of form and movement is comparable to the finest examples of Buddhist painting at Tun-huang. The suggestion of a swaying, dancing rhythm, appropriate to the iconography of the Dākinī, is imparted not only by the gentle torsion of the slim body, corseted in a scaled cuirass, but also by the long fluttering scarves, streaming like pennons in the wind to fill more than half the wall space allotted to the figure of the Dākinī herself. These windblown ribbons cannot fail to remind us of the similar use of such motifs in the famous scroll attributed to Ku K'ai-chih (ca. A.D. 400), "The Admonitions of the Instructress of the Palace Ladies," in the British Museum. FIG. 75
The painting of draperies stirring and moving as though a wind were in them is attributed to the great Wu Tao'tzu by the T'ang historians of painting in their descriptions of Master Wu's now-vanished masterpieces in contrast to the soaked, clinging draperies characteristic of the Soghdian artist Ts'ao Chung-ta. Again, in this particular frieze from Turfan, the isolation of the figures against the empty background reflects this compositional device in the classic Chinese mode of figure drawing as seen in the scroll by Ku K'ai-chih and the works of early T'ang masters like Yen Li-pên. Likewise, the color scheme in its combination of ochers, greens, and tawny browns is a distinctly T'ang palette.

The penetration of Manichaeanism into China is attested by textual evidence, such as the dispatch of a "Teacher" as an envoy of the king of Chaganian to the T'ang court in A.D. 719, and by the finds at Khocho of fragments of sacred texts and votive portraits of noble devotees of the faith. In the example illustrated, although realistic portraiture is intended, the formula for the massive bearded head and the hieratic pose echo the Chinese-type portraits of the early T'ang period, as in Yen Li- PLATE P. 195

Fig. 77 – Eleven-headed Avalokitesvara (Juichimen Kannon). Kondo of the Horyuji, Nara, Japan. Compare p. 191.

FIG. 76 pên's famous Scroll of the Thirteen Emperors. As in the mural of Buddhist friars from Shorchuk, the circular designs of the robes are still vaguely Sasanian in derivation. The actual type and purely linear treatment of these noblemen may remind us of the striking likenesses of the ambassadors at Afrasiab, but here the more stereotyped treatment of the figure has replaced the delicate naturalism of draftsmanship characterizing the portrayals of the envoys at Samarkand.

An illustration of the cosmopolitan religious and artistic atmosphere of the Turfan region in the ninth century is provided by a fragmentary PLATE P. 196 mural believed to represent a Nestorian religious ceremony. The differentiation between the Western type of the priest and his obvious East

Asian congregation is a kind of realism we have not previously encountered in Central Asia. Although certain technical details, like the
fine linear expression and the blank background, are suggestive of Chinese practice, other details, like the abstract greenish shading of the
priest's robe and the whole feeling of the panel, crude but direct in nar-
rating a religious scene, are haunting reminiscences of the Late Antique
mode of Early Christian art and Byzantium, a style completely apart from
the Indo-Iranian idiom of Kucha and the Chinese tradition of Turfan.
This fragment, like the Nestorian remains from Khocho, clearly indicates
that each separate religious group, represented in these missionary outposts, perpetuated something of the artistic traditions of its distant
origins in the Roman East and Iran.

Typical of the predominant Mahāyāna iconography and style of Turfan
is the fragment of a banner representing the Eleven-headed Avaloki-   PLATE P. 197
teśvara. This esoteric form of the Bodhisattva of Compassion is known in
many examples of T'ang sculpture and painting. A wooden image of this
deity of the tenth century or earlier was found at Toyuk. The present
example is an illustration of the kind of classical perfection developed in
T'ang China on the basis of Indian models. The conception in rounded
volumes stressed by the rhythmic repetition of the curved lines describing
the outline and interior drawing of the features gives an air of rarefied
purity, the T'ang adaptation of the Gupta formula to volumes even more
abstract in simplified geometric circular shapes. In the process all suggestion of the Indian expression of sensuous warmth and sensuality has
been refined away. Although the rounded lines may suggest spheroidal
mass, the expression is essentially composed in terms of line and flat tone
through the traditional Chinese mode of calligraphic, even cursive, draftsmanship. This fragment, a not undistinguished example of the mature
T'ang style of Buddhist painting, is comparable to the probably somewhat earlier representation of the Eleven-headed Avalokiteśvara in
one of the badly damaged eighth-century wall paintings of Hōryūji at
Nara (Fig. 77).

The graveyard of Astana in the Turfan oasis yielded a treasure trove of
textiles and fragments of painting to both the Japanese expeditions and
the excavation of this site by Sir Aurel Stein. The fragments of woven silk
include the boar's head medallion (Plate 15), which is probably of pure
Sasanian origin, and, among the Japanese finds, are fragments of the
favorite Sasanian emblem of the winged horse, which are possibly of
eastern Iranian origin or local imitations of this originally Zoroastrian
motif.

PLATE P. 198The fragmentary paintings found at the site obviously date from a period when the art of the Turfan oasis, like the decorations of the Tun-huang grottoes, was a provincial extension of Chinese painting of the T'ang period. In the collection of the National Museum in New Delhi are fragments of scroll paintings on silk, painted in a courtly style representing ladies and attendants under flowering trees. The famous painting of Court Ladies Preparing Newly Woven Silk by the T'ang painter Chang Hsüan, which we know only in a copy attributed to the Sung emperor Hui Tsung,[3] belongs to this same school, which derives from the T'ang court painter Chou Fang, known by a copy of a similar subject of court ladies listening to music.[4] The Astana painting exhibits the same T'ang ideal of soft, voluptuous beauty, painted in brilliant colors, with the forms set off against a background of empty silk. This same figure style is represented by other eighth-century masterpieces, like the Kichijōten of Yakushiji at Nara [5] and the screens with paintings of ladies under trees in the Shōsōin treasury.[6] The fragments of the scroll in New Delhi are without doubt an imported example of this style to Turkestan. These soft beauties in the serenity of this budding grove are a small but exquisite Central Asian reflection of the golden luxury of the short moment of grandeur in the civilization of T'ang China.

1. *Scythian, Persian and Central Asian Art from the Hermitage Collection* (Catalogue, in Japanese), Tokyo, 1969, p. 7.
2. S. Beal, *Life of Huien-tsang*, pp. 18, 21.
3. Sherman, E. Lee, *A History of Far Eastern Art*, New York, (no date), p. 339.
4. *Ibid.*, p. 290.
5. *Ibid.*, Fig. 346, p. 273.
6. *Ibid.*, Fig. 347, p. 273.

The figure, with the exception of some small indication of shading in the folds of the robe, is presented entirely in terms of the virtuoso line drawing typical of the T'ang period. The mask of the Buddha is the same formalized stereotype, again entirely linear in expression, which appears over and over again in the wall paintings recovered from this site by Stein and von Le Coq. The color scheme with its predominant reds and greens is a tonality frequently encountered in the wall paintings of Tun-huang.

In Vajrayāna, or Tantric Buddhism, the Five Dākinīs, like the Five Tāras, are the female counterparts or consorts of the Five Dhyāni Bodhisattvas. They are sometimes described as fiends or the manifestations of Kālī. Their pacific and angry aspects are reflected in the three heads of the examples from Bezäklik. They are sometimes associated with the more orgiastic rituals of Tantric Buddhism, exerting their charms to arouse excesses of lust to provide a cathartic subjugation of evil impulses. Their attributes include the noose, the sacrificial knife, the skullcap, and the vajra. Their presence at Bezäklik may be taken as evidence of the strong Tibetan influence that began to infiltrate Buddhism and the art of Turfan and Tun-huang in the eighth century.

Kneeling Buddha. Detail of a Pranidhi legend. Wall painting from Shrine XII, Bezäklik, Turfan, Chinese Turkestan. W. 21½ in. 9th century A.D. *Museum for Central Asian Antiquities, New Delhi.*

Dākini. Wall painting from Bezäklik, Turfan, Chinese Turkestan. 8th–9th century A.D. *Museum of Central Asian Antiquities, New Delhi.*

194

Portrait of a Uighur Prince. Fragment of wall painting, Temple 19, Bezäklik, Turfan, Chinese Turkestan. H. 55 cm. 8th–9th century A.D. *Indische Kunst Abteilung, Staatliche Museen, Berlin (Dahlem)*.

A Uighur inscription reads in part: "This is the god-like portrait of the prince Alp drslan." The nobleman is represented between parted curtains, wearing a miterlike headdress (perhaps a Manichaean crown) and holding a flower as an offering to the shrine.

"Palm Sunday." Wall painting from the Nestorian temple from the eastern gate, Khocho, Chinese Turkestan. H. 23½ cm. 9th century A.D. *Indische Kunst Abteilung, Staatliche Museen, Berlin (Dahlem)*.

This fragment of wall painting shows a robed priest holding a chalice before a group of worshipers of obvious Mongol type. They hold what look more like the branches of fruit trees than palms. The principle of hieratic scaling prevails in the difference in size between the priest and the congregation.

One explanation of this esoteric form of the Bodhisattva of Compassion is that when Avalokiteśvara looked down on the miseries of the world, his head literally split with pain, and his spiritual father, the Buddha Amitābha, refashioned these fragments into eleven separate heads, some benevolent, others malignant in expression. Nine heads are visible in the fragment in our illustration. According to a different iconographical explanation, three heads express rage at the evil of the world; three rejoice in the good; and three are filled with compassion for man's sorrows. The crowning head of the Buddha Amitābha appears at the top of the Turfan painting. The left hand is raised in the *vitarka mudrā*.

196

Eleven-headed Avalokiteśvara (Ekadaśamukha Avalokiteśvara). Fragment of painting on silk. From Turfan. H. 14 cm. 8th century. *Indische Kunst Abteilung, Staatliche Museen, Berlin (Dahlem).*

Detail of Ladies and Attendants under Flowering Trees. Fragments of painting on silk from Astana, Chinese Turkestan. 8th century A.D. *Stein Collection, National Museum, New Delhi.*

X. THE THOUSAND BUDDHA CAVES OF TUN-HUANG

THE ART OF THE SILK ROAD AND THE FAR EAST

The last stage on the long road from western Central Asia to the gates of China proper was the oasis of Tun-huang at the end of the lines that constituted the western end of the Great Wall. Although the region of Tun-huang in present-day Kansu Province came under Chinese rule as early as the first century of our era, the actual foundation of the famous Thousand Buddha Caves (Ch'ien Fo-tung) is traditionally associated with the monk Lo-ts'un, the holy man from the "Western Countries," who excavated the first sanctuaries in the loess cliff in the year A.D. 366. As is specifically mentioned in the *Wei shu,* "The land of Tun-huang, from its relations with the religious and laity of the Western Countries, obtained from them prototypes for stupas and Buddha images." A later inscription of the year A.D. 776 relates that "first the Thousand Images of the Thousand Buddhas of the *kalpa* of the virtuous were modeled in moist clay, which was then painted with various colors; spaciously the walls of the shrines were freed from the rock; majestically the golden faces of the Buddhas assumed their shapes" — a description that would be equally valid for the procedure followed in the sites of the "Western Countries," from which the artists of Tun-huang drew their inspiration.

The stylistic character of the surviving painted and sculptured decorations of the Six Dynasties period reveal the closest connections with the styles at Kizil and other sites on the northern trade route. Before A.D. 439, when the territory was taken by the T'opa Tartars of the Northern Wei dynasty (A.D. 386–534), Tun-huang had been the domain of the Liang people. The Liang rulers, sometimes of Tibetan, sometimes of Chinese origin, maintained a precarious, ephemeral dominion in Kansu Province as early as the late fourth century. The kings of the so-called Northern Liang dynasty, founded in 410, were ardent patrons of Buddhism. Following the invasion of the T'opa Tartars in 439, the population of Kansu was enslaved and deported to the Wei capital at Ta T'ung-fu. It is quite possible that Liang artisans, trained at Tun-huang, may have had a part in fashioning the images in the cave temples of Yün Kang begun in 450.

Although it used to be assumed that all the early work at Tun-huang perished during the persecution of Buddhism from A.D. 446 to 453, many Western as well as Far Eastern scholars are now of the opinion that at least some of the earliest surviving wall paintings and sculptures at Tun-huang escaped this iconoclastic movement and may be dated in the Northern Liang period (A.D. 412–439), or slightly later. In this connection, the earliest dated inscription of A.D. 538 is located in Cave 285 (Cave 120 according to the numbering system of Paul Pelliot).

A single example will serve to show the close relationship between Tun-huang and the Kucha oasis. In a number of the earliest caves, the modeled clay Buddha statues reveal a drapery formula in which the originally classical garment has been reduced to a series of flat, tapelike folds arranged in meaningless forked folds ("Gabel Falte") over the torso and limbs (Ill. 34). This convention, originally appearing in late Gandhāra statues from Pāitāvā (Ill. 2) and Shotorak, is presented as a completely formalized pattern in a fragment from Kizil (Fig. 78). It makes its appearance, too, in some of the earliest Chinese rock-cut statues of the later fifth century, notably the attendant Buddha image of Cave 22 at Yün Kan (ca. A.D. 450–494) (Ill. 35) and the bronze Maitreya of A.D. 477 in the Metropolitan Museum, New York.[1]

It should be noted that, even in the earliest caves at Tun-huang, where Central Asian influence predominated, there was beginning to emerge that purely Chinese style of Buddhist sculpture, which in its hieratic abstraction and dematerialization of the forms into linear symbols of divine beings, is a process closely approximating the similar abstract formulas to suggest the transcendental and invisible in the Romanesque period. The special factors of this Six Dynasties style, such as the conception of the heads as cubic masses and the elongation and flattening of the bodies, are mystical rather than decorative in intent.

One of the earliest wall paintings at Tun-huang of the Six Dynasties period will serve admirably to illustrate the transference of Central Asian styles, notably the manner associated with Kucha, to this Chinese Buddhist frontier post. This is the representation of the Ruru Jātaka, dealing with the Bodhisattva's incarnation as a stag, in Cave 257 (Pelliot, 110). PLATE P. 207 Although the serrated-mountain conventions and the flowerlike trees are inherited from the technique of the Han reliefs, many elements take us back to the styles we have followed over the Silk Road from Western Central Asia; for example, the batiklike quality of the deer outlined against the red background reminds us of the famous stenciled ram textile of the Shōsōin (Fig. 79), itself an ultimate reflection of the heraldic style of Sasanian Iran. Like the Chinese imitations of Sasanian textile patterns found at Astana, the Shōsōin ram batik is probably a production of the seventh century, when the flight of the Sasanian nobility, together with Persian craftsmen, broke in a wave of Iranian influence over China. We have encountered the floral conventions that fill the background of the Tun-huang Deer Jātaka at Kizil and Bāmiyān. Even though the red ground of the Tun-huang mural may have an iconographical significance — a symbolic reference to the red earth of the Gangetic plain where the legend took place — its decorative combination with the stylized beast forms evokes memories of the hunting frescoes of Varaksha. The human PLATE P. 70 figures in their proportions and the technique of reinforcing the outlines with heavy bands of tone can be found in numerous examples at Kizil, PLATE P. 161 and the trailing serrated scarves of the kneeling suppliant before the stag repeat a convention we have seen in the beautiful Celestial Musician and Deva at Kizil. Below the frieze of the Jātaka story is a zone with an illu- PLATE P. 159 sionistic portrayal of parallelepipeds, just as we see them in the wall paintings of Bāmiyān and in Roman mosaics at Shāpur and elsewhere (Fig. 80). The wall painting of Cave 257 in its extraordinary combination PLATE P. 207 of forms from the Western countries and earlier indigenous traditions is a perfect example of the fusion of these Central Asian and Chinese elements into the Six Dynasties style. Again, the wall paintings of many of the early caves at Tun-huang reveal a color scheme with predominant blue and green tonality tones that closely approximate the palette of the Indo-Iranian manner at Kizil.

It is only in the Six Dynasties caves of the fifth and sixth centuries at Tun-huang that we can rightly speak of the intrusion of Central Asian styles, as we have seen in the decorations of Cave 257, from the Kucha region. In some of the other early grottoes, for example, Cave 428, the scenes of Buddha preaching, flanked by Bodhisattvas and Devatās, the schematized shading of the bodies in heavy outlines of orange vermillion pigment (sometimes oxidized to a dark brown color), are a further sim-

PLATE P. 171

plification of the already patternized Indian chiaroscuro at Kizil.[2] There are similar technical reminiscences of the Kizil style in the Jātaka stories on the ceiling decorations of the same cave, but the arrangement in long scroll-like bands is certainly a Chinese contribution; and the archaic trees and sharply pointed, flat mountain motifs that separate the consecutive scenes, although vaguely reminiscent of the merlon conventions found at Kizil, are surely adaptations of primitive landscape formulas already employed in Han reliefs and metalwork. Again, in Cave 285, dated A.D. 538, the painted ceiling is completely Chinese in style, but the representation on the walls flanking the niche of the central Buddha image in a galaxy of Hindu divinities, including Maheśvara, Vishnu, Ganesha, and Kumara,[3] clearly reflects those provincial translations of the Indian style that we have seen at Bāmiyān and in many details at Kizil. Except for these portrayals of the Hindu titans which would appear to represent a kind of primitive mandala assimilating the Brahmanic deities as symbols of the Buddha's manifold powers, the early sculpture and painting at Tun-huang are largely Hinayāna in character, and this iconography in itself would indicate an affiliation with Kucha and other Buddhist sites on the northern trade route.

In all the later grottoes at Tun-huang from the seventh century onward, the oasis and its art swing completely into the orbit of T'ang China, a moment in art history that saw the formation of a truly classic Chinese art. This was the period of the great masters of painting, Yen Li-pên, Wu Tao-tzu, and Wang Wei. The part played by Central Asian painters, like Wei-ch'ih I-sêng of Khotan and Ts'ao Chung-ta of Samarkand, has already been mentioned. There is a legend that the latter brought a painting of "Amitābha and the fifty Bodhisattvas" from his homeland, the subject of which may have provided the basis for the iconography of "The Paradise of Amitābha" in Cave 322 at Tun-huang.[4] The international character of T'ang Buddhist art was furthered by the closer contacts with the Western countries through the travels of Hsüan-tsang, the pilgrim, and Wang Hsüan-tsê, the imperial envoy. It was undoubtedly this new and more direct contact with India of the late Gupta and post-Gupta period

Fig. 79 – Ram. Batik on silk. Shosoin, Nara, Japan. Compare p. 201.

that was responsible for the more distinctly plastic, voluminous form in T'ang Buddhist sculpture, the discarding of the old hieratic and angular shapes of Six Dynasties icons in favor of an expression in swelling, rounded volumes and softly undulating drapery, both revealing the massive Indian forms and enhancing the suggestion of their fullness and ponderosity. The new realism and dynamic movement in religious painting and sculpture is part of this Chinese Renaissance, a reflection of the spiritual and material power of the Middle Kingdom. The westward expansion of this new Chinese idiom has already been noted in the art of the last centuries of artistic activity in Turfan. The force of this ascending tide of Chinese styles was checked by the final occupation of all of Central Asia by Islamic invaders in the tenth century.

The beginnings of landscape painting in China as a setting for Buddhist subjects already found in examples of the Six Dynasties wall paintings at Tun-huang have, as we have seen in the examination of the Ruru Jātaka of Cave 257, only slight connections with Central Asia. It is part of that Chinese humanist romantic interest in man's environment that is the poet's and painter's involvement in the mysteries of nature, and is a completely indigenous development.

The art of Tibet and Nepal is artistically as well as geographically outside the scope of the present work. There are many records of Khotanese painters working in Tibet, but our earliest examples of Tibetan painting and sculpture, both from Turfan and Tun-huang, appear like local, often imaginative, adaptations of Indian prototypes of the Pāla-Sena period (ca. 750–1197), together with an assimilation of Chinese techniques and decorative forms. The Lamaist art of Mongolia and China is a transference of the Tantric style of Lhasa to the Far East.

What can we say of Central Asian art in comparison with the art of the Eastern world as a whole for the period of something more than a millennium that we have followed its development? It goes without saying that the remains of painting and sculptures found in the skeletal ruins of these many vanished civilizations from the Caspian Sea to the gates of China are of the greatest importance for our knowledge of the spread and growth of Buddhist iconography. They help to complement what we know of the linguistic and ethnic character of the many different peoples that once brought these civilizations to flower. The intensive scientific work of the Russian archaeologists in the ancient provinces of Transoxiana, taken in connection with the remarkable finds in the ruined palaces and monasteries of this desert tract, present a complete picture

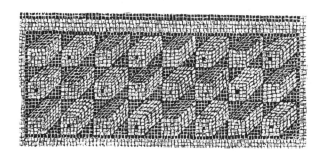

Fig. 80 – Mosaic with parallelepipeds, from Bishapur, Iran. Louvre, Paris. Compare p. 201.

of the material culture of these lands. This is not true of the results of the excavations, or, perhaps better, "prospecting expeditions," in Serindia carried out sporadically and often under tremendous difficulties by German, British, French, Japanese, and Russian expeditions before China barred any further explorations in Sinkiang after 1915.

From the aesthetic point of view, the names of a handful of famous masters from Soghdiana and Khotan are mentioned in Chinese sources, and we have a few copies remotely recalling their exotic styles. For the most part throughout all Central Asia as in ancient India and Iran, painting and sculpture are an anonymous craft tradition, often carried out, we may suppose, by bands of workers like the Magistri Comacini of the later Middle Ages in Italy. Often the work strikes us as routine and mechanical in performance. Excluding the few fragments of Chinese origin buried in the graves of Astana, is there anything to which we can apply the word "masterpiece" in the way that this encomium is freely awarded to Western artists of all periods? What most nearly approaches the definition of monumental and magisterially composed are the cycles of the legend of Rustam at Pyandzhikent and the splendid composition of the ambassadorial suite at Afrasiab, which, in narrative energy, arrangement, and, of course, draftsmanship and color, evoke memories of some of the great fresco complexes of our Western heritage, such as the Triumph of Death at Pisa, or even the Giottesque murals at Assisi. As we have seen, a single fragment, the Harpist of Pyandzhikent, rivals the exquisite grace of Trecento Siena and Heian Japan. Certainly the exotic Mannerist sculpture of Fondukistan can be placed beside the best of late Gupta and Pāla art. Although, as at Kizil, there are flashes of what we can recognize as the expression of aesthetic pleasure in the pure beauty of color able to communicate an appropriate divine luminosity, it has to be admitted that a great deal of the remains of sculpture and painting in Serindia is mediocre in comparison with the art of the great civilizations that surrounded the wastes of innermost Asia.

There are, of course, many exceptions in sculpture to the judgment that so much of this material is mere repetitive artisan plasterers' work, as in the notable fragments from the Kucha oasis and Shorchuk, illustrated in this book. Again, although there are great variations in the competence of the painters of Kizil, there are many unforgettable individual panels such as the Devatā and Gandharva and the astonishing portrayals of the chevaliers of Kuchaglow with the splendor of Byzantine mosaics.

Just as the famous treasure of Begram reveals a collection of luxury goods from the Graeco-Roman, Iranian, Indian, and Chinese worlds gathered in the palace of the Kushan emperors, so the fabulous contents of the Shōsōin at Nara, bequeathed to Tōdaiji by the Emperor Shōmu in 753, presents an incredible inventory of treasures, many of which found their way to Japan over the ancient Silk Road. In this connection, it must not be forgotten that Central Asia by its strategic geographical, commercial, and political position at the heart of Asia was not only the recipient of the iconography and techniques of all the great empires of the pre-Islamic East — Hellas and Rome, Iran, the empire of the Kushans, and India of the great classical periods — but also the transmitter of these traditions that formed the cornerstone of the great Buddhist cultures of China, beginning in the Six Dynasties period, and ultimately shaped the religious and material culture of Japan from the days of Shōtoku Taishi to the final magnificence of Buddhist art in the Heian and Kamakura periods.

1. L. Sickman and A. Soper, *The Art and Architecture of China,* 2nd edition, Baltimore, 1960, Pl. 30(A).
2. Pelliot, *op. cit.,* Pl. CCLXXXII.
3. *Ibid.,* Pl. CCLXI, CCLXV.
4. Pelliot, *op. cit.,* V, Pl. CCCXVIII.

Ruru Jātaka. Wall painting, Cave 257, Tun-huang, China. 5th–6th century A.D.
The wall painting illustrates the story from one of the former lives of the Buddha, when in his incarnation as a magnificent golden stag he saved a merchant from drowning in the Ganges. This miscreant reported the presence of the wondrous deer to the king of Banares. The wall painting represents the confrontation between the royal hunter and his intended prey, and the rajah's submission to the eloquent preaching of the golden stag against the taking of life. The picture unfolds according to the old principle of continuous narration, whereby consecutive episodes of a story are contained within the same frame, proceeding from the original rescue of the informer from the river to the submission of the king before the miraculous deer.

207

1. Buddha. From Mardan, Gandhara, Northwest Pakistan; 1st–2nd century A.D. *Photo Archaeological Survey of India, Lahore. Compare p. 28.*
2. The Buddha of the Great Miracle. Paitava, Afghanistan. *Kabul Museum, Photo B. Rowland. Compare p. 28.*
3. Bodhisattva. Gandhara, Northwest Pakistan; 1st–2nd century A.D. *Royal Ontario Museum, Toronto. Photo museum. Compare pp. 29, 98.*
4. Putti with garlands. Detail from a wall painting. Hadda, Afghanistan. *Musée Guimet, Paris. Photo museum. Compare p. 37.*
5. Flying divinites. Wall painting from the niche of the 53-meter-high Buddha, Bāmiyān. *Copy by A. Godard, photo Musée Guimet, Paris. Compare p. 106.*
6. Ivory rhyton from Nisa (detail); 2nd century B.C. *Hermitage, Leningrad. Photo Josephine Powell, Rome. Compare p. 47.*
7. Gilt silver dish. Bactrian; 2nd century B.C. *Hermitage, Leningrad. Photo museum. Compare p. 48.*
8. A and B: Obverse and reverse of a tetradrachma of Demetrius of Bactria. From the Kunduz Treasure; 2nd century B.C. *Kabul Museum.*
   C: Tetradrachma of Eucratides of Bactria (obverse); 2nd century B.C. *Kabul Museum. Photos J. Powell. Compare p. 48.*
9. River goddess, from Pendzhikent, U.S.S.R.; 7th–8th century A.D. *Hermitage, Leningrad. From A. M. Belenitskij and B. Pitrovskij: Skul'tura i dzhivopis' drevnogo Pyandzikenta, Moscow, 1959, plate XXX. Compare p. 63.*
10. Capital from Chamquala; 1st century B.C. or later. *Kabul Museum. From B. Dagens, M. le Berre, D. Schlumberger: Monuments préislamiques d'Afghanistan, MDAFA, XIX, Paris 1964, plate XXIV, 1. Compare p. 52.*
11. Statue of a princess, from Chamquala, U.S.S.R.; 4th–5th century A.D. *Photo J. Powell. Compare p. 55.*
12. Charred wooden statue of a prince. From Pendzhikent, U.S.S.R.; 7th–8th century A.D. *Hermitage, Leningrad. Photo J. Powell. Compare p. 61 ff.*
13. Torso of a Bodhisattva. From Adzhina Tepe, U.S.S.R.; 7th–8th century A.D. *Dushanbe Museum. Photo Prof. B. A. Litvinskij, Dushanbe, U.S.S.R. Compare p. 78.*
14. Tribute bearer or envoy. Wall painting from Afrasiab, Samarkand; 6th–7th century A.D. *From V. A. Shishkin: Afrasiab, Tashkent, 1966, p. 19. Compare p. 71*
15. Banquet scene (detail). Wall painting from Balalik Tepe, U.S.S.R. *From G. A. Pugachenkova and. L. I. Rempel: Istoriya iskussv' Uzbekistana, Moscow, 1965, fig. 12. Compare pp. 68, 73 mm., 94.*
16. Head of a prince. From Toprak Kala, U.S.S.R.; 4th–5th century A.D. Hermitage, Leningrad. Photo J. Powell. Compare p. 54
17. Head of a prince. From Khalchayan, U.S.S.R.; 1st century B.C.–1st century A.D. From G. A. Pugachenkova: *La sculpture de Khalchayan, in Iranica Antiqua, vol. 2, 1065. Compare pp. 49 ff., 55.*
18. Head of a Bodhisattva. Gandhara, Northwest Pakistan. 1st–2nd century A.D. *Philadelphia Museum of Art. Photo-Museum. Compare p. 51.*
19. Bust of a female harp player. From Airtam, U.S.S.R.; 1st century A.D. or earlier. Hermitage, Leningrad. Photo J. Powell. Compare pp. 49, 51.
20. Head, from Varaksha, U.S.S.R.; 6th century A.D. or later *Hermitage, Leningrad. Photo J. Powell, Compare p. 74.*
21. Bamiyan Valley, Afghanistan. (With 35-meter-high Buddha.) *Photo B. Rowland. Compare p. 83.*
22. Thirty-five-meter-high-Buddha. Bamiyan. *Photo B. Rowland. Compare p. 84.*

6

7

8 a

8 b

8 c

9

10

11

12

13

14

15

16

17

18

19

20

21

22

23

24

25

26

27

28

29   30   31

32

33

34

35

23. Bodhisattva Avalokiteshvara. Wall painting from Ajanta, Cave I. *From G. Yazdani: Ajanta, I. Oxford, 1930, plate XXXI. Compare pp. 99, 102.*

24. Bejeweled Buddha. Fondukistan, Afghanistan. *Musée Guimet, Paris. Photo museum. Compare p. 118.*

25. Nagini, or water spirit. Wall painting and statue of the Vaisravana. From Dandan-Uilik, Khotan, Chinese Turkestan; circa 5th–6th century A.D. *From F. H. Andrews: Wall-painting from Ancient Shrines in Central Asia, Oxford, 1948, plate XXXII. compare pp. 127, 130.*

26. The Great Miracle of Sravasti (or Vairocana-Buddha). From the Rawak Stupa, Khotan, Chinese Turkestan. *From Sir M. A. Stein: Ancient Khotan, Oxford, 1907, p. 492. Compare p. 126 ff.*

27. Indian statue. Painting on silk. Tunhuang, China; circa 8th century A.D. *National Museum, New Delhi, Slg. Stein. From Sir M. A. Stein: The Thousand Buddhas, London, 1921, plate XIV. Compare p. 126.*

28. Relief from Tumshuk, Chinese Turkestan; 6th century A.D. or later. *Musée Guimet, Paris. Photo museum. Compare p. 141 ff.*

29. Head of a Bodhisattva, from Tumshuk, Chinese Turkestan; 5th century A.D. or later. *Musée Guimet, Paris. Photo museum. Compare p. 142.*

30. Head of a Bodhisattva. Kumtura, Chinese Turkestan. 5th century A.D. or later. *State Museums, Prussian Cultural Property, Museum for India Art, Berlin. Photo museum. Compare 168.*

31. Head of a Bodhisattva. Mathura; circa 4th–5th century A.D. *Muttra Museum. From L. Hambis: Toumschouq, I. Paris, 1961, plate CXXXVIII, 392. Compare p. 142.*

32. Relief. Ming-oï, Shorchuk, Chinese Turkestan; 6th century A.D. or later. *From Sir M. A. Stein: Serindia, III, Oxford, 1921, fig. 295. Compare p. 175.*

33. Pranidhi scene. Bäzäklik, Turfan, Chinese Turkestan. *Formerly State Museums, Prussian Cultural Property, Ethnological Museum, Berlin. Photo museum. Compare p. 182.*

34. Seated Buddha. Tunhuang, Cave 257; circa 500 A.D. *Photo Langdon Warner. Compare p. 200.*

35. Buddha. Yuen Kang, Cave 22; 450–494 A.D. *From O. Sirén: Chinese Sculpture, II, London, 1925, plate 54. Compare p. 200.*

	GREECE AND ROME	IRAN	RUSSIAN TURKESTAN
400 B.C.			
	332 B.C. Alexander routs the Persians in battle of the Issus River 364–322 Seleucid Empire	331 B.C. Invasion of Alexander; fall of Achaemenid Empire 323 Death of Alexander 364–321 Seleucid Empire	329–327 B.C. Alexander in Soghdia and Bactria
300 B.C.		250 Parthian Empire	
200 B.C.	159–133 Kingdom of Pergamum 146 Fall of Corinth	173–138 Mithridates I 123–88 Mithridates II	Hellenistic art of c. 173 B.C Old Nisa or Mithridatkart c. 160 B.C. Kushans (Yüehchih) in Ferghana
100 B.C.	64 Roman conquest of Syria 31 Egypt a Roman province 27 B.C.–A.D. 14 Augustus	53 Parthian victory over Romans at Carrhae	
0	98–117 A.D. Trajan		Palace of Khalchayan Sculpture of Airtam-Termez
A.D. 100	117–138 Hadrian 161–180 Marcus Aurelius		
A.D. 200	260 Capture of Valerian by Shapur I	241–273 A.D. Shapur I Reliefs of Naqsh-i-Rustam; Bishapur 276–293 Varahran II Revival and reformation of Zoroastrianism by Kartir	Buddhist shrine at Giaur Kala (Merv)

AFGHANISTAN	INDIA AND PAKISTAN	SERINDIA	CHINA
	327–325 B.C. Alexander's march to the Indus 322–185 Maurya Empire		
250 B.C. Bactrian kingdom under Diodotus c. 220 Euthydemus of Bactria 200 Siege of Bactria by Antiochus III City of Ay-Khanum	273–233 Asoka		Ordos Animal style 206 B.C.–A.D. 25 Former Han dynasty
166-136 Eucratides c. 130 Fall of Greek Bactrian kingdom	185–80 Sunga period		165 B.C. Yüeh-chih driven from Kansu by Hsiung-nu 138–126 General Chang Ch'ien's mission to Ferghana and Bactria 121 General Ho Ch'ü- ping defeats the Huns
Treasure of Begram	Kujula Kadphises W'ima Kadphises	73 B.C. General Pan Chao in Khotan	2 A.D. Kushan (?) Buddhists in China 25–206 Later Han dynasty
Beginning of Gandhāra art 110–115 A.D. Kanishka Kushan sanctuary of Surkh-Kotal	Beginning of Gandhāra art 110–115 A.D. Kanishka Kushan capitals at Peshawar and Mathura		148 Parthian Buddhist teacher An Ehih-kao in China 181 Parthian Buddhist teacher An Hsüan in China
242 Invasion of Shapur I and fall of Great Kushan dynasty			
			265–581 Six Dynasties period

	GREECE AND ROME	IRAN	RUSSIAN TURKESTAN
A.D. 300	307–337 Constantine 330 Founding of Constantinople 359 Siege of Amida by Shapur II	309–379 Shapur II	Buddhist stupa at Merv
A.D. 400			Toprak Kala (Khwarezm)
	476 Fall of Rome	484 Death of King Peroz in battle against the Hephthalites	
A.D. 500	527–565 Justinian	529–579 Khusrau I 590–628 Khusrau II Taq-i-Bustan Grotto of Taq-i-Bustan	Balalik Tepe Varaksha
A.D. 600		613–651 Arab conquest of Iran 642 Battle of Nehawand	651 A.D. Capture of Merv by Arabs Pyandzhikent Afrasiab Adzhina Tepe 674 A.D. Arab advance into Transoxiana
A.D. 700			722 Fall of Pyandzhikent to the Arabs 739 Samarkand and all of Soghdia under Arab dominion
A.D. 800	800 Carolingian Empire		
A.D 900			
A.D. 1000			

AFGHANISTAN	INDIA AND PAKISTAN	SERINDIA	CHINA
Hadda			
	320–600 A.D. Gupta period		366 A.D. Tun-huang founded by Lo-ts'un 395–414 Fa Hsien's pilgrimage
		4 A.D. Khotán (Rawak Vihāra, etc.)	440 Northern Liang in Turfan 439 T'opa Tartars conquer Liang territories
450 A.D. Devastation of monasteries of Nagarahara and Hadda by White Huns	450 Invasion of White Huns Ajanta, Cave I Buddhist sculpture of Mathurā and Sārnāth		450–494 Yün Kang cave temples 494 Northern Wei capital at Loyang Lung-mên cave temples
		Tumshuk Kizil-Kucha	
Bāmiyān			
	606–647 Harshavardhana	640 Turfan occupied by Chinese	618–906 T'ang dynasty 627–649 T'ai Tsung
632 Arab conquest of Bactria Kakrak Fondukistan		647 Kucha occupied by Chinese 670 Tibetan conquest of Khotan, Kucha, Karashahr, and Kashgar 692 Chinese expel Tibetans	625–645 Hsüan-tsang's pilgrimage 632–635 Chinese domination of Serindia Wei-ch'ih I-sêng, Khotanese painter 640–680 Yên Li-pen
	c. 730–1197 Pāla and Sena dynasties in Bengal	Shorchuk 753–840 Uighur Kingdom in Turfan 790 Tibetan conquest of Turfan	751 Defeat of Chinese by Arabs at Talas
		Moslem domination of Serindia	906–960 Five Dynasties period 960–1279 Sung dynasty

BIBLIOGRAPHY

ABBREVIATIONS

CR   *Central Asian Review*
CRAI   *Comptes rendus de l'académie des inscriptions et belles lettres*
ICCAKP *International Conference on ... the Culture of the Kushan Period,* Dushanbe, 1968
JISOA   *Journal of the Indian Society of Oriental Art*
MDAFA *Mémoires de la délégation archéologique française en Afghanistan*

GENERAL

Akiyama, T. *Musée Guimet:* Museums of the World. Kodansha, Tokyo, 1968.

Beal, S. *Buddhist Records of the Western World.* London, 1906.

(Fa Hsien), *Travels of Fa Hsien* ... 395–414 A.D. Edited by H. A. Giles, Cambridge, 1923.

Franz, H. G. *Buddhistische Kunst Indiens.* Leipzig, 1965.

Frye, R. N. *The Heritage of Persia.* London, 1963.

Ghirshman, R. *Persian Art: 249* B.C.–651 A.D. New York, 1962.

Goetz, H. *India, Kunst der Welt.* Baden Baden: Holle Verlag, 1959.

Grousset, R. *In the Footsteps of the Buddha.* London, 1932.

Mongait, A. *Archaeology in the USSR.* Moscow, 1959.

Rice, T. T. *Ancient Arts of Central Asia.* New York, 1965.

Rowland, B. *The Art and Architecture of India.* 3d ed. Baltimore, 1967.

Seckel, D. *Kunst des Buddhismus.* Baden Baden: Holle Verlag, 1962.

Waldschmidt, E. *Gandhāra, Kutscha, Turfan.* Leipzig, 1925.

Wheeler, Sir M. *Rome Beyond the Imperial Frontiers.* London, 1954.

II. GANDHĀRA

Bachhofer, L. *Zur Datierung der Gandhāra Plastik.* Munich, 1925.

Barthoux, J. "Les fouilles de Hadda: Figures et figurines." MDAFA, VI. 1930.

Barthoux, J. "Les fouilles de Hadda: Stupas et sites." MDAFA, IV. 1933.

Buchthal, H. "Foundations for a Chronology of Gandhāra Sculpture." *Transactions of the Oriental Ceramic Society,* 1942/43. London, 1944.

Deydier, H. *Contribution à l'étude de l'art du Gandhāra.* Paris, 1950.

Faccena, D. *Sculptures from the Sacred Area of Butkara, I.* Rome, 1962.

Foucher, A. *L'art gréco-bouddhique du Gandhāra.* 2 vols. Paris, 1905–18.

Ingholdt, H. *Gandhāra Art in Pakistan.* New York, 1957.

Marshall, Sir J. H. 3 vols. *Taxila.* Cambridge, 1951.

Marshall, Sir J. H. *The Buddhist Art of Gandhāra.* Cambridge, 1960.

Meunié, J. "Shotorak." *MDAFA,* X. 1942.

Rowland, B. *Gandhāra Sculpture from Pakistan Museums.* New York: Asia Society, 1960.

III, VI–IX. SERINDIA

Akiyama, T. "The Painted Dado of Shrine M.V. at Mirān," *Bijutsu Kenkyū,* 212, Sept., 1960.

Andrews, F. H. *Wall Paintings from Ancient Shrines in Central Asia.* 2 vols. London, 1948.

Arnold, Sir T. W. *Survivals of Sasanian and Manichaean Art in Persian Painting.* Oxford, 1924.

Bussagli, M. *Painting in Central Asia.* Geneva: Skira, 1963.

Grünwedel, Albert. *Bericht über archäologischen Arbeiten in Idikutschari* (Abhdlg. d. Hist. Classe ... bayer. Akad. d. Wiss., XXIV, I. Abt.), München, 1909.

Grünwedel, Albert. *Altbuddhistische Kultstätten in Chinesisch-Turkistan.* Berlin, 1912.

Grünwedel, Albert. *Alt-Kutscha.* Tafelwerk, Berlin, 1920.

Hallade, M. "Indo-Iranian Art." *Encyclopaedia*

of *World Art*, VIII. New York, 1963.

Hambis, L. "Asia, Central." *Encyclopaedia of World Art*, I. New York, 1958.

Hambis, L. *Toumschoug*. 2 vols. Paris, 1961 and 1966.

Hambis, L. "Khotanese Art." *Encyclopaedia of World Art*, VIII. New York, 1963.

Hambis, L. "Kucha." *Encyclopaedia of World Art*, VIII. New York, 1963.

Hatani, R. "Buddhist Art in Central Asia." *Monumenta Serindica*, V. Kyoto, 1962.

Klementz, D. *Turfan und seine Altertümer: Nachrichten über die ... im Jahre 1898 ausgerüsteten Expedition nach Turfan*. St. Petersburg, 1889.

Kumagai, N. "A Painted Casket from Kucha." *Bijutsu Kenkyū*, 191. March, 1957.

Kumagai, N., and others. "The Ancient Buddhist Arts in Central Asia and Tun-huang." *Monumenta Serindica*, V. Kyoto, 1962.

Le Coq, Albert von. *Chotscho*. Berlin, 1913.

Le Coq, Albert von. *Die buddhistische Spätantike in Mittelasien*. 7 vols. Berlin, 1922–33.

Le Coq, Albert von. *Bilderatlas zur Kunst und Kulturgeschichte Mittel-Asiens*. Berlin, 1925.

Le Coq, Albert von. *Buried Treasures of Chinese Turkestan*. London, 1928. [Translation of *Auf Hellas Spuren*, Leipzig, 1926.]

McGovern, W. M. *The Early Empires of Central Asia*. Chapel Hill, 1939.

Pelliot, Paul. "Mission en Turkestan chinois." *CRAI*. Paris, 1910.

Pelliot, Paul. *La Haute Asie*. Paris, 1931.

Rice, Tamara T. *Ancient Arts of Central Asia*. New York, 1965.

Stein, Sir M. A. *Sand-buried Ruins of Khotan*, Oxford, 1903.

Stein, Sir M. A. "Explorations in Central-Asia, 1906–08." *Geographical Journal*, 34, 1909.

Stein, Sir M. A. *Ancient Khotan*. Oxford, 1907.

Stein, Sir M. A. *Ruins of Desert Cathay*. 2 vols. London, 1912.

Stein, Sir M. A. *Ancient Chinese Figured Silks Excavated ... at Ruined Sites of Central Asia*. Reprint from *Burlington Magazine*. London, 1920.

Stein, Sir M. A. *Serindia*. 5 vols. Oxford, 1921.

Stein, Sir M. A. *Innermost Asia*. 4 vols. Oxford, 1926.

Stein, Sir M. A. *On Ancient Central-Asian Tracks*. London, 1933.

Ueno, T. "Sculpture of Chinese Turkestan." *Monumenta Serindica*, V. Kyoto, 1962.

IV. RUSSIAN CENTRAL ASIA AND BACTRIA

Al'baum, L. I. *Balalik Tepe*. Tashkent, 1960.

Belenitskii, A. *Central Asia*. Archaeologia Mundi. Geneva, 1968.

Belenitskii, A., and others. *Zhivopis' i skul'tura Drevnego Pyandzhikenta*. Moscow, 1959.

Curiel, R., and Fussman, G. "Trésors monétaires d'Afghanistan." *MDAFA*, XIV. Paris, 1953.

Curiel, R., and Fussman, G. "Le Trésor monétaire de Qunduz." *MDAFA*, XX. Paris, 1965.

Frumkin, G. I: "Archaeology in Soviet Central Asia and Its Ideological Background." *CR*, X, 4, 1962, pp. 334–342.

Frumkin, G. II: "Kazakhstan." *CR*, XI, 1, 1963, pp. 13–29.

Frumkin, G. III: "Kirgiziya and the Fergana Valley." *CR*, XII, 1, 1964, pp. 16–29.

Frumkin, G. IV: "Tadzhikistan." *CR*, XII, 3, 1964, pp. 170–184.

Frumkin, G. V: "The Deltas of the Oxus and Jaxartes: Khorezm and Its Borderlands." *CR*, XIII, 1, 1965, pp. 69–86.

Frumkin, G. VI: "Uzbekistan, Excluding Khorezm." *CR*, XIII, 3, 1965, pp. 239–257.

Frumkin, G. VII: "Turkmenistan." *CR*, XIV, 1, 1966, pp. 71–89.

Frumkin, G. *Archaeology in Soviet Central Asia*. Handbuch der Orientalistik, III, 1, Leyden, 1969.

Gafurov, B. *Kushan Civilization and World Culture*. ICCAKP. Moscow, 1968.

Gardner, P. *The Coins of the Greek and Scythic Kings of Bactria and India in the British Museum*. London, 1886.

Hallade, M. "Bactrian Art." *Encyclopaedia of World Art*, II. New York, 1960.

Hallade, M. "Indo-Iranian Art." *Encyclopaedia of World Art*, VIII. New York, 1963.

Hambis, L. "Khwarezm." *Encyclopaedia of World Art*, VIII. New York, 1963.

Hambis, L. "Soghdiana." *Encyclopaedia of World Art*, XIII. New York, 1967.

Litvinskii, B. A. *Outline History of Buddhism in Central Asia*. ICCAKP. Moscow, 1968.

Lukonin, V. *Iran II*. Archaeologia Mundi, Geneva, 1967.

Masson, M. E., and Pugachenkova, G. A. *Parfyanskie ritony Nisy*. Moscow, 1956.

Narain, A. K. *The Indo-Greeks*. Oxford, 1957.

Pugachenkova, G. A. *Khalchayan*, Tashkent,

1965.

Pugachenkova, G. A. *Iskusstvo Turkmenistana.* Moscow, 1967.

Pugachenkova, G. A., and Rempel, L. I. *Sstoriya iskusstv' Uzbekistana.* Moscow, 1965.

Rice, T. T. *Ancient Arts of Central Asia.* New York, 1965.

Schlumberger, D. "Descendants non-méditerranéens de l'art grec." *Syria,* XXXVII, 1960, pp. 142ff.

Shishkin, V. A. *Varaksha.* Moscow, 1963.

Shishkin, V. A. *Afrasiab.* Moscow, 1966.

Smirnov, I. I. *L'argentérie orientale.* Moscow, 1940.

Staviskii, B. Y., and Bongard–Levin, G. M. *Central Asia in the Kushan Period.* ICCAKP. Moscow, 1968.

Staviskii, B. Y., and others. *Sovietskaya arkheologiga Srednei Azii i Kushanskaya problema.* ICCAKP. Moscow, 1968.

Tarn, W. W. *The Greeks in Bactria and India.* Cambridge, 1953 and 1966.

Tolstov, S. P. *Drevnii Khorezm.* Moscow, 1948.

Tolstov, S. P. *Po drevnim deltam Oksa i Yaksarta. Moscow,* 1962.

Trever, K. V. *Pamyatniki Greko-baktriyskogo iskusstva [Monuments of Greco-Bactrian Art.]* Moscow and Leningrad, 1940.

Yakubovskii, A. Yu, and others. *Zhivopis' drevnego Pyandzhikenta.* Moscow, 1954.

V. AFGHANISTAN

Bussagli, M. "Afghanistan." *Encyclopaedia of World Art,* I. New York, 1958.

Dagans, B., Le Berre, M., and Schlumberger, D. "Monuments préislamiques de l'Afghanistan. *MDAFA,* XIX, 1964.

Foucher, A., and Bazin–Foucher, Mme. E. "La vielle route de L'Inde de Bactres à Taxila." *MDAFA,* I, 1942–47.

Ghirshman, R. "Les Chionites-Hephthalites." *MDAFA,* XIII, 1948.

Godard, A. and Y., and Hackin, J. "Les antiquités bouddhiques de Bāmiyān." *MDAFA,* II, 1928.

Hackin, J., and Carl, J. "Nouvelles recherches archéologiques à Bāmiyān." *MDAFA,* III, 1933.

Hackin, J. and J. R. *Le site archéologique de Bāmiyān: Guide du visiteur.* Paris, 1934.

Hackin, J., and others. "Diverses recherches archéologiques en Afghanistan." *MDAFA,* VIII, 1959.

Mizuno, S., Casal, J. M., Rowland, B., Schlumberger, D., and Yoshikowa, L. *Ancient Art of Afghanistan.* Tokyo, 1964.

Rosenfield, J. M. *The Dynastic Arts of the Kushans.* Berkeley and Los Angeles, 1967.

Rowland, B., and Coomaraswamy, A. K. *The Wall-paintings of India, Central Asia, and Ceylon.* Boston, 1938.

Rowland, B. "Buddha and the Sun God." *Zalmoxis,* I, 1938.

Rowland, B. "The Dating of the Sasanian Wall-paintings at Bāmiyān and Dukhtar-i-Noshirvan." *Bulletin of the Iranian Institute,* VI–VII, 1946.

Rowland, B. "The Colossal Buddha at Bāmiyān." *JISOA,* XV, 1947.

Rowland, B. "The Bejewelled Buddha in Afghanistan." *Artibus Asiae,* XXIX, 1, 1961.

Rowland, B. *Ancient Art from Afghanistan.* New York, 1966.

Schlumberger, D. "Le temple de Surkh Kotal en Afghanistan." *Journal Asiatique,* 1952, p. 433; 1954, p. 161; 1955, p. 209.

Wheeler, Sir M. *Flames over Persepolis.* New York, 1968.

X. TUN-HUANG

Gray, B. *Buddhist Cave Paintings at Tun-huang.* London, 1959.

Matsumoto, E. *Tonko-gan no Kenkyu* [Study of the Tun-huang paintings.] Tokyo, 1937.

Pelliot, P. 6 vols. portfolios. *Les grottes de Touen Houang.* Paris, 1914–24.

Sawa, R. "Frescoes of the Tun-Huang Cave Temples." *Monumenta Serindica.* Kyoto, 1962 (in Japanese).

de Silva, A. *Chinesische Landschafts-Malerei am Beispiel der Höhlen von Tun-huang.* Kunst der Welt, Holle Verlag, Baden-Baden, 1965.

Stein, Sir M. A. *The Thousand Buddhas.* London, 1921.

Waley, A. *A Catalogue of Paintings Recovered from Tun-huang by Sir Aurel Stein.* London, 1931.

INDEX

The numerals in italics refer to the plates and figures

226